52

About the Adizes Methodology

When we began hearing about Ichak Adizes from various company presidents we knew and respected...they simply said that he was a new breed of management consultant, one who really understood how businesses work and what could be done to make them better. Adizes is, in fact, more than a consultant. He is a pioneer in the field of management — a serious, insightful, and astute observer of organizational behavior, which he has been studying for 25 years.

The Editors of Inc. magazine

In the past year we have increased sales by 70%, reduced operating costs, increased profitability and have significantly improved the climate in our organization. There is no question that much of the credit for this belongs to the Adizes methodology.

Donald D. Boroian, President
Francorp, Inc.

The mutual respect and enthusiasm that developed was incredible. Adizes gave me the vehicle and the impetus to get participation pushed throughout the company. There's no doubt that the change in climate was substantial...his method allows you to get from everyone what they are capable of contributing.

Frank Chamberlain, President
Porter Paint Company

People exhibit different characteristics at different periods in their lives; so do corporations. Dr. Adizes articulates these stages as no one has done before; he will provide you with insights about your corporate organization that will make you immeasurably wiser.

William F. Farley, Chairman
Farley Industries

With Ichak, we examined our management structure to find ways to give more focus and definition, and come up with an organization chart...It was absolutely successful! We went in somewhat skeptical and came out exhilarated. We gained a great deal of focus and gained individual as well as team responsibility.

Ernest Fleischmann,
Executive Vice President & Managing Director
Los Angeles Philharmonic

The Adizes methodology has helped us solve many structural and functional problems. I believe it is the most advanced management methodology in the world today.

P.N. Gerolymatos, President
P.N. Gerolymatos S.A., Greece

Adizes has helped us think as a corporation. Before, each of us acted to represent his own division. Now we operate as a team.

Fernando Hilsenbeck, Vice President
Villares Industries, Brazil

Ichak has simplified management theory. His message is clear and concise...Like reading Peter Drucker, the more time you invest in Mastering Change the higher your return on investment.

George Landgrebe, President and CEO
American Banker/Bond Buyer

Ichak Adizes is a management guru — and his insights are as applicable to personal life as they are to management...In this book you will find, as I have, the benefits of a full, well–rounded theory that is practicable in daily life.

Harvey Mackay
Author of the best seller
How to Swim with the Sharks and Not Get Eaten

Adizes is one of the few management consultants who has converted a whole array of theory–based concepts into unusually practical guidelines for managers. And even more impressive, he has integrated these guidelines into a comprehensive system of management. Furthermore this tour de force is centered on a lifecycle concept that zeros in on a widespread source of management difficulties.

William H. Newman, Professor Emeritus
Columbia University Graduate School of Business

Dr. Adizes' methodology not only provides an extraordinarily effective means to build a functionally effective organizational structure, his approach...allows functional changes...to occur in a morale–building environment.

Loren Rothschild, President
American Protection Industries, Inc.

The Adizes Executive Development Program gave me new and effective ways to deal with persistent and difficult management decisions.

Lee Ruwitch, Publisher
Miami Review

The experience has been extremely good. People attending the different Phases...are all convinced that the methodology is a good one, and that the amount of time spent in the sessions is worthwhile...The people seem to be more confident in the future of the company. Everything seems to be happening together. As we are going through these exercises, we are building up internal confidence and internal trust. The people are calmer and know that we are better prepared for the future.

Paulo Villares, President and CEO
Villares Industries, Brazil

Reading and re–reading Adizes not only stimulates innovative thinking, but directs effective action. How uncommon is his common sense approach to complex situations.

Kirby Warren, Professor
Columbia University School of Business

MASTERING CHANGE

MASTERING CHANGE

*The Power of Mutual Trust and Respect
in Personal Life, Family Life, Business and Society*

Ichak Adizes, Ph.D.

*Adjunct Associate Professor
John E. Anderson Graduate School of Management
University of California at Los Angeles*

*Founder and Professional Director
Adizes Institute
Santa Monica, California*

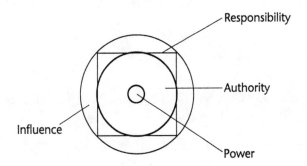

Adizes Institute Publications

MASTERING CHANGE
The Power of Mutual Trust and Respect
in Personal Life, Family Life, Business and Society

Copyright © 1991 by Ichak Adizes

Printed in the United States of America

10 9 8 7 6 5 4 3 2 1

Library of Congress Catalog Card Number: 91–76029
ISBN 0-937120-04-9

Adizes Institute Publications

Jacket design by Larry Didona
Book design by Timothy McIndoo

*Dedicated to the Certified Adizes Practitioners worldwide,
without whom the contents of this book could not be a reality.*

Contents

Acknowledgments

The list of people who contributed to this book is quite long. I have been lecturing about this material for twenty–five years. It started as a small simple model and it grew over time as people came forward and made remarks[1]. Some disagreed and enriched me with their disagreements. Some reinforced my presentation and contributed anecdotes, jokes, case histories, even cartoons. Over time I realized that what was applicable to the organizations I was lecturing about applies to personal life too. When I was invited to speak to heads of state and their cabinets, the applicability of the material on the social–political plane became evident as well.

So, whom do I thank? Where do I start? Certain people stand out. First, my parents, who through their Sephardic Jewish wisdom taught me much about life. Outside my family, Mr. Vukadinovic, my first grade teacher in Belgrade, Yugoslavia, stands out for a lesson I will not forget. I was an eight year old child saved from the Holocaust, in which half of my family perished. I was scared and timid. Another child in the class harassed me publicly with anti–Semitic insults. Mr. Vukadinovic put us both in front of the class and lectured us about brotherhood, how we look the same, yet still can enjoy the beauty of being different. He spoke about trust and respect. He had us sit at the same desk for the rest of the year, and my enemy became one of my best friends, remaining so to this day. Next, I want to thank Yehuda Erel, my youth leader in the Israeli Noar La Noar youth movement. I came to Israel after World War II, looking for a home, full of fears of being rejected. He gave me roots and a sense of belonging by teaching me to serve others who were less fortunate than myself.

Then came my years of study in the United States. Professor William H. Newman of Columbia University taught me management theory, but more important than that, he taught me with his open mindedness and practical outlook on the management process, an approach to intellectual life which I try to emulate.

Last, but not least, for the past three years I have been learning from interactions with my friend Amrit Desai (also known as Gurudev), the spiritual leader and founder of the Kripalu Center in Lenox, Massachusetts. From him I am learning about love of oneself, about harmony and integration with the world which surrounds us.

Not to be overlooked are Rosemary Sostarich, Adrienne Denny, Elspeth MacHattie, Charles Mark, Bill Chickering, Michael Lame, and Denise Reiss. Each helped shape this book, whether by reviewing, editing, or retyping it. To all, thank you.

To each of my teachers, associates, and students I offer my deepest appreciation and thanks.

Ichak Adizes
Santa Monica, California
September, 1991

About the Author

Dr. Ichak Adizes (Yitz–hak Ah–dee–zes) has applied his theories of mastering change for twenty–five years in 35 countries with over four hundred organizations, with business corporations as well as with not–for–profit organizations, that range in size from 80 employees to 90,000 employees. Furthermore, he has been invited by heads of state to lecture to ministers and members of parliament about his theories and practice and to consult on how to debureaucratize government.

Dr. Adizes is the Founder and Professional Director of the Adizes Institute in Santa Monica, California. The Institute is dedicated to the training and certification of Adizes Practitioners, and to applying the Adizes methodology for solving managerial problems through consulting to organizations with Certified Adizes Practitioners located in twelve countries.

Dr. Ichak Adizes is an Adjunct Associate Professor at the John E. Anderson Graduate School of Management at the University of California in Los Angeles and he has held teaching appointments at Columbia University, Stanford University, Tel Aviv University, and the Hebrew University in Jerusalem. He also has been a member of the American Sociological Association, the International Sociological Asociation, the American Political Science Association, and the Academy of Management. His four previous books have been translated into thirteen languages.

A sought–after lecturer who is fluent in four languages, his work has been featured in *Fortune, Inc.*, the *New York Times*, the *London Financial Times*, and many other major foreign publications.

Dr. Adizes was born in Yugoslavia and raised in Israel. He received his BA from Hebrew University in Jerusalem, his MBA and PhD degrees from Columbia University in New York City.

He practices yoga, loves folk dancing and playing the accordion for a sing–along. He and his two sons reside in Brentwood, California and Tel Aviv, Israel.

The Meaning of Management

One afternoon I was talking with a student of mine. He was intelligent and intellectually curious. He wanted to learn what I knew about management that enabled me to teach and lecture worldwide. He asked if I would take the time to talk about my field of expertise. I liked his curiosity and offered to answer his questions. As we walked in the park exchanging questions and answers, this book took shape in my mind.

I understand that you have been studying the process of management and leadership for more than twenty years. What is it?

First we have to define what the word *manage* means.

The Traditional Theory of Management
I've found that in certain languages, such as Swedish, French, and Serbo–Croatian, "manage" does not have a literal translation. In those languages, words like *direct, lead,* or *administer* are often used instead. When they mean to say "manage" in the way we use it in the United States, they usually use the English word. In Spanish, for example, the word *manejar,* the literal translation for "manage", means "to handle" and is used only

1

when referring to horses or cars. When they want to say "manage" in the American sense of the word, they use *direct* or *administer*.

But isn't the process universal?

No. In certain countries the managerial process, as it is practiced in the United States and taught in its business schools, is prohibited by law. In the Yugoslav self–management system, if a manager made a unilateral decision for a company, he could be criminally prosecuted. It would be considered a negation of the democratic process. Instead, a manager had to "suggest," while the workers decided. In Israel, the secretary of a kibbutz, who holds a managerial position, is periodically re–elected so that no one can claim permanence in governing others.

You mean the kibbutz secretaries manage for a while and then go back to milking the cows?

Or to serving in the dining room or washing dishes. Management is not permanent there, just as no elected government is permanent. That would negate democracy. They are not managers by profession.

What, then, is management, if some languages don't have a direct translation and some sociopolitical systems negate it or practically forbid it? Would the synonyms in the dictionary provide a sufficient definition?

Well, what synonyms would you suggest?

"Decide," "operate," "plan," "control," "organize," "rule," "achieve goals," "lead," "motivate," "accomplish"...

In several dictionaries the synonyms for "manage" are the ones you have mentioned. There are other intriguing synonyms, like *dominate* and *govern*, from the American Collegiate Dictionary. The Oxford Dictionary adds *manipulate* and *connive*. Interestingly enough, none of the dictionaries I looked at listed *lead* or *motivate* as synonyms.

I don't like the synonyms "connive" and "manipulate".

And for a very good reason. Let's see what that reason is by analyzing the common denominator shared by all the synonyms we've mentioned, excluding *lead* and *motivate*. Imagine the process described by each of these words. Animate their meaning. Can you identify the common denominator? *Operate...plan...control...organize...rule...achieve...accomplish.*

> *They are all a one–way process. The managing person is telling the managed person what to do. The manager determines what should be done and the managed person is a means of accomplishing that end.*

That's why we call a manager the "head" of the department, and a valued subordinate is called the "right hand." The right hand does exactly what the head tells it to do, while the left hand behaves as if it had a will of its own. It is not fully controllable.

> *But managers are also called supervisors.*

Because a supervisor is supposed to have *superior vision*. Look at the insignia for military officers. You can compare the progressive ranks represented by United States' military insignia to climbing a tree and then ascending to the sky. The lieutenants have bars representing the branches of a tree. The captain has two bars; he is going up the tree. The major has a leaf representing the top of the tree. Then the colonel soars like an eagle, and the general has a star. The higher they go up the organizational hierarchy, the better their vision should be. The problem with such a philosophy is the lowliness of the subordinates. The lower they are on the tree, the less they can see and are allowed to know. Listen to the word: subordinates. They are *sub–ordinary.*

> *If the manager is called the superior, then are the staff people called inferiors?*

In Hebrew, subordinates are literally called "bent," as if the managers had molded them to do whatever they wanted.

> *This is a bit upsetting.*

It is upsetting because the managerial process, as it is taught and practiced is not a value–free process. It is not only a science and an art, but also an expression of sociopolitical values. It is a value–loaded *political* process.

> *Didn't we leave out "motivate" and "lead"? Don't these synonyms redeem the process of management from what appears to be its hierarchical, one–way–street connotation?*

In that context, what is the meaning of the words *lead* and *motivate*? Isn't the connotation that, as a manager or leader, I know what I want the subordinates to do? The challenge is finding the way to lead and motivate them to do it. If I can't control, maybe I can motivate. What does that sound like?

> *Manipulation.*

Right! I remember a cartoon in the *New Yorker* magazine. A mother who is a psychologist is trying to convince her son to take out the trash. Wearily, the boy says, "OK, OK! I'll take out the trash, but pleeeease, Mom, don't try to motivate me." Even the child sees motivation as a manipulation. What he must do has already been decided. It's only a matter of how to make him do it. Should it not seem strange that labor unions often oppose programs such as job enrichment or enlargement, which management uses to motivate workers? Labor views these programs as ploys to increase productivity and profitability for the good of management. The only benefit to the workers is that they may keep their jobs.

The same connotation of manipulation comes up in the synonym *lead*. Some theories of leadership, if you read them carefully, discuss leadership not as the process of deciding *what* needs to be done and *why*, but rather on *how* to make the followers follow. Should the leader direct the followers or discuss the decision with them? That can be seen as a manipulation because the leader does not have to care about what the followers genuinely need. In some industries management is a dirty word. In the arts in the United States, it is often synonymous with exploitation.

> *So what do you suggest?*

The Functionalist View

We have to understand the role of management by the function it performs: *why* do we need it? And the function should be value–free, without any sociopolitical or cultural biases. It should be the same, whether we are managing ourselves, our family, a business, a nonprofit organization, or a society. Whether we speak of managing, parenting, or governing, it should be one and the same process conceptually. The only difference would be the size and nature of the unit being managed.

This sounds very ambitious. Where do we start?

Do you agree with one thing, that change is constant? The process has been going on since the beginning of time and will continue forever. The world is changing physically, socially, economically. Even you are changing this very minute. Change is here to stay.

Yes?

And change creates problems.

Yes.

And problems require solutions.

Yes.

And solutions create more changes. We can diagram the sequence like this:

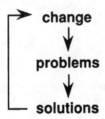

Now if change is here to stay, what else is here to stay?

Problems.

And the greater the quantity and velocity of the changes, the greater the quantity and complexity of the problems we will have.

The point is that people should not expect to permanently solve all problems. When one set of problems is solved, a new generation of problems will emerge. We will stop encountering problems only when there is no more change, and that will happen only when we are...

Dead.

Right! Living means solving problems, and growing up means being able to solve bigger problems.

The purpose of management, leadership, parenting , or governing is exactly that: to solve today's problems *and* get ready to deal with tomorrow's problems. This is necessary because there is change. No management is needed when there are no problems, and there are no problems only when we are dead. To manage is to be alive, and to be alive means to experience change with the accompanying problems it brings.

Then how do we manage change?

I suggest that managing change involves two processes. First, you must decide what to do, and then...

You have to implement your decisions.

Right. For managing well, both processes are necessary, and together they are sufficient. So our diagram of the management process looks like this:

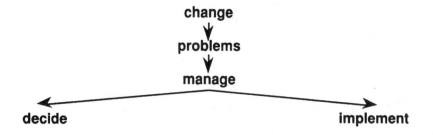

And these processes are value–free. You can apply them to manage anything from a criminal underworld to a community of saints. Whenever there is change, you must make decisions and you must carry out those decisions.

> *But are both factors really necessary? Some people hate to decide. It's too painful. Do they have to decide?*

Not deciding, or procrastinating, *is* a decision. They cannot escape the fact that whenever there is change, they must make a decision, or the change itself will de facto make the decision for them. And while making a decision is necessary, it is not sufficient. They also need to implement the decision.

To manage well, you need both to make good decisions and to implement them efficiently. You are not managing well if you make bad decisions that you implement well or if you make good decisions that you implement badly.

> *Wait! Why is the implementation factor separate? Shouldn't implementation follow naturally if the decision is a good one? As a matter of fact, a decision is not a good one unless it includes a plan of implementation. Thus, all that is needed for managing is to make outstanding decisions. Period.*

It's not so simple. Look at your personal life. How many decisions have you made that you never implemented? Even though you sat down and made a list of exactly what you would do, you still did not implement the decision.

Do you smoke? Or maybe you overeat? Since you know both activities are bad for you, you've probably decided to change these habits. Yet you probably still go on behaving the same way despite a detailed plan to implement change.

> *You mean I'm not in control of my life?*

Are you? Have you implemented all the decisions you've made to change?

> *No, I have not. I'm still struggling with losing some weight. I've made the decision to change my diet many times, but have never*

succeeded in doing it. It's embarrassing.

The same holds true for almost any organization. Management might decide to change direction, markets, product line or the culture of the organization. It has great difficulty implementing such changes. The same phenomenon occurs in the governing of countries. Many leaders, even dictators, complain that their decisions involving change do not get implemented. For instance, Hitler could not force the implementation of his decision to burn Germany in front of the advancing Allied forces. His decision was never carried out, although he had total power to execute anyone who didn't follow his orders.

> *Both factors, decision–making and implementation, are necessary for managing change, and both factors are sufficient. If I want to solve problems and manage well, whether it's my personal life, career, family, organization or society, I must make good decisions and then implement those decisions efficiently.*

Yes, and as your experience with dieting shows, the quality of the decision can neither predict nor assure the probability of implementation. Some decisions that require change, even if they are outstanding, do not get implemented; and some bad decisions, like smoking or overeating, get implemented swiftly.

Why is that?

It's because the two processes, decision making and implementation, are incompatible. It's as if you were holding two books. One book tells you how to make good decisions, the other tells you how to implement decisions. If you follow the instructions on how to make good decisions, those instructions will undermine your efforts to implement the decisions efficiently. And if you follow the instructions on how to implement efficiently, they will undermine your capability to make good decisions.

I'd understand that better if you gave me an example.

Look at political systems. Which system is designed to increase the probability of making good decisions? Which system fosters open discussion and vehemently protects the freedom of information, speech and the press so that good decisions can be made?

Democracy.

That's right. And have you noticed how difficult it is in a democracy to implement public policy decisions that require change? The system may make good decisions, but the legitimate political dissension necessary to make the decision becomes a stumbling block in implementation. Most leaders in democratic systems complain their policies don't get implemented as swiftly as they would like.

Now, which political system allows quick implementation of decisions by not allowing discussion, dissension or questions?

A totalitarian system.

Yes. And totalitarian regimes usually make bad decisions. Why? Because efficient implementation is carried out by forbidding freedom of the press, dissension and discussion. It's "do it or else." This inhibits the exchange of information necessary to form educated judgments. Instead of quality decisions, such regimes often produce biased decisions with horrible outcomes.

Are you saying that good management is democracy in decision making and dictatorship in implementation?

Correct! In personal life it means that in order to make a good decision, you must be open minded. You must operate democratically within your own mind and with other people. But once a decision is made, you must become dictatorial, which in personal life means you must commit to the decision, be strong–willed, and carry it through.

That's easier said than done.

Absolutely. Democracy in decision making and dictatorship in implementation is what I call "democratship." It is a difficult process. Many people mismanage by having it upside–down: they're dictatorial in decision making and democratic in implementation.

That's me, I think. I'm dictatorial in deciding to lose weight. "I have made up my mind absolutely. There will be no more discussion. This is final," I say. And I remain resolute until the sandwiches arrive. I then conveniently turn democratic and heed the voices of dissension.

You've got the idea, my friend. You must have democracy and dictatorship in the right sequence. You must be capable of being democratic and then dictatorial, and the difficulty is in the word *then*. When do you stop being democratic and start becoming dictatorial? When do you quiet the voices of dissension? Some people are democratic in decision–making and continue being so during implementation. They're inefficient because they keep changing their decision. On the other hand, resolute people carry out efficient implementation, but their closed minds hurt the decision–making process. They're difficult to reason with because they don't listen well. They end up making decisions based on inadequate or biased information. In contrast to the democratic style, which is effective but not efficient, the totalitarian style is efficient but not effective.

Do you mean to say that democracy is not an efficient system?

Yes, I do. If you try to make it an efficient political process, it will lose its effectiveness.

By the same token, are you saying that totalitarian regimes cannot be effective? Come to think of it, they're not. The Soviet economy, in its central planning mode, has difficulty producing according to plan–it even has food shortages.

Totalitarian regimes are ineffective. The more democratic they become, the more effective they can be.

But then they'd have to give up some political efficiency.

Yes, and that's not easy. People usually want something more without losing what they have. They prefer "more" to "instead of."

To manage, lead, parent, or govern well means to decide and implement, to be democratic, then dictatorial. This is very tricky, It's tricky not only in managing a business, but in family and personal management as well. It's one reason why the managerial process is so difficult.

You must decide and implement, be open–minded and resolute at different times. You have to know which frame of mind is correct at which time. Defined this way, the managing process is all–encompassing, universal, and value–free.

$$\text{quality of management} = f \left\{ \begin{array}{l} \text{1. quality of decisions;} \\ \text{2. efficiency of implementation.} \end{array} \right\}$$

I think I've got it. Both factors are necessary, and together they are sufficient. The better our decisions and the more efficient our implementation, the better we manage. But how do we make those good decisions and implement them efficiently? How do we measure the quality of decisions? I could analyze a decision after the fact and say, "That was a good decision." But isn't analysis after the fact too late?

That is an excellent subject for our next conversation. Tomorrow? Same time, same place?

Sure. See you soon, and thank you.

Conversation 2

Predicting the Quality of Decisions

Now, where were we?

You said that the quality of management, leadership, parenting, or governing depends on the quality of the decisions made and on the efficiency of implementation. Today we were going to discuss how to make good decisions.

Let's start. In order to make a good decision, we need to know how to *predict* the quality of a decision. We don't want to analyze a decision after it's been implemented, and then judge it by its success or failure.

But how do you do that?

Let's use an example. Let's say we have a write–up of a problem or a case that contains all the information necessary to diagnose and solve the problem. Let's assume we give that case to a group of four people. These four people don't know anything more about the case than what's presented in the write–up. They have no additional information beyond that.

We ask them to study the problem together and devise the solution. They are instructed to write down both the problem and the solution, seal the result inside an envelope and return it to us.

Now let's take another group of four people and give them the same assignment. They too have no additional information beyond what's written up. They have the same case and the same assignment. After the two groups complete their task, we have two sealed envelopes.

Now, are we going to find that these envelopes contain the same problem and the same solution?

No. Most likely they will contain different problems and different solutions.

Right, but why? The case is the same. Both groups have exactly the same information. Why are the problems and solutions different?

Because the people are different!

You have just discovered the key factor in the managerial or leadership process! In order to manage well you have to manage the *people* who write what is in the envelope instead of managing the problem itself that is in the envelope. There are managers who say, "I love to manage. It's people I can't stand!" If you do not like working with people, you are in the wrong profession. Too many managers, leaders, or parents of grown–up children say, "Give me the envelope." They open it and say, "Wrong problem! Wrong solution! The right problem and the right solution are..." They think they are managing, leading, or parenting, when what they are really doing is just working hard. Even if they accept what is written in the envelope, how do they know they have found *the* right problem and *the* right solution?

But if they're the managers, they should know better than their employees. That's why they get paid more, isn't it? Isn't that why leaders get elected?

They *should* know better, but do they? Is getting paid more an assurance that a person knows more? Does a leader necessarily know more?

Then why is the manager getting paid more? What do we reward leaders for?

It's not for knowing more about *the* problem or *the* solution. They should get paid more for knowing how to find the right people, the "knowledgeables," and for managing them to the right answer. If a manager claims to know everything, the organization is in trouble.

If managers want to have the right problem and the right solution, they must match the right people to the case at hand. They must create the environment which will enable these people to arrive at the right problem and the right solution.

But as a leader or manager, how do I recognize the real problem and the real solution? How do I distinguish the right problem and solution from the wrong ones? If I don't necessarily know more than the people I lead or manage, then how do I evaluate their decision? I could make a mistake, right?

To know whether the people are proposing a good decision or not, you must ask two questions. If the answer is yes to both questions, you have the right problem and the right solution. If the answer is no to either of the two questions, you have the wrong problem and the wrong solution.

What are the questions?

To understand what those two questions are will take several conversations. At the beginning, our conversations may seem somewhat complicated and overly academic. Later, the usefulness and applicability of these concepts and how they can lead to the answers to those two questions will become clear.

I 'm ready. Let's proceed!

The Four Roles of Decision–Making

No decision is made in a vacuum. It is made to achieve something. A decision is good if it achieves the desired results. The quality of a decision should be evaluated in light of the impact it has on the system for which it was made. Thus, if a decision can make an organization both effective and efficient in the short and the long run, the decision is a good one.

Now we'll discuss the characteristics of a good decision that will cause an organization to be effective and efficient in the short and long run. We can present it as a chart:

input ⟶ output	
four decision roles	**organizational characteristics**
•	effective ⎫ short
•	efficient ⎭ run
•	effective ⎫ long
•	efficient ⎭ run

I've studied management practices in several countries and have observed what happens under different conditions. I was like the British naval doctor who, from an isolated ship, observed that when people's diets are deficient in vitamin C, they develop scurvy. I studied management practices in countries where certain managerial roles were forbidden by law, and I observed and analyzed the managerial "diseases" that emerged.[2] By doing that, I identified the necessary characteristics, the four "vitamins" which I call the "decision roles" that produce healthy organizations, organizations that are effective and efficient in the short and the long run. When any one of the roles is missing, a pattern of corresponding mismanagement will occur.[3] I can analyze and predict the outcome of a decision by analyzing which roles are being performed and which ones are missing.

You mean to say that anytime one of the roles is missing, typical mismanagement will occur. And that by knowing which role is missing, you can predict whether the organization will be mismanaged and whether it will be ineffective and/or inefficient in the short and/or the long run .

That's correct.

Then you can look at managerial problems as you would diseases, identify which missing role caused them, inject the missing role, or roles, into the system, and lead the organization back to health.

Yes! I look at an organization as a total system and at what makes it "healthy" or "sick." I solve specific problems by treating a total system. I call this the Adizes methodology. The Adizes methodology offers a holistic theory of management, both therapeutic and preventive. One company, for instance, helped by this methodology and other factors has increased sales from $12 million to $750 million in sales in ten years without any dilution of ownership.[4]

Another company grew profitably from $150 million to $2.5 billion in sales in ten years and again without any dilution of ownership.[5]

Is the benefit permanent?

It can be if the company is constantly nourished and nurtured by repeatedly using the methodology. Otherwise, in the long run, the methodology's effectiveness will diminish, and eventually the organization will lose the benefits. It's like exercising or eating right.

Can anyone do it?

If properly trained.

How different is it from what traditional consultants do?

We do not prescribe medicine, meaning we do not write consulting reports. We empower the organization to release and utilize its own energies to take care of itself. We coach the organization to generate those "vitamins" so it can stay healthy without further intervention from us. Typical consultants do not teach you how to stay healthy. Usually you need continuous periodic infusions of their consulting services. This methodology is different. While helping the organization change, it simultaneously empowers it to handle future problems so it doesn't develop an addiction to outside intervention. It teaches the organization how to manage itself correctly and continuously.

I'm interested in hearing more. What are the four roles?

Short and Long Run Effectiveness
First, a decision must make the organization effective. If the decision doesn't produce effectiveness, then the decision is not a good one.

What does "effective" mean?

In the short run an organization is effective if its immediate short–run actions are functional.

What do you mean by "functional"?

A decision is functional when it satisfies the immediate needs for which it was made. Whenever we make a decision, we have an objective. We want to accomplish something. Hammering a nail is functional if it hammers in nails. We do not, however, hammer nails for nothing. There must be a purpose. Let's say we are constructing a cabinet. We have needs we want to satisfy, problems we want to solve. Hammering the nail a certain way so that it goes in properly is short term effectiveness. Continuously hammering so that a cabinet is produced is long term effectiveness. If the decision we made to hammer nails and/or build a cabinet does not satisfy the needs or solve the problem, then the decision doesn't work.

Give me another example.

When you read a book you have expectations about what you will get out of it. If reading the book doesn't satisfy your expectations, you might feel you wasted your money and time. It's the same with marriage. We marry somebody because we have certain needs and expectations. If those expectations are not satisfied, we might feel we made the wrong decision, we married the wrong person. The marriage is not functioning. Every decision, whether we are aware of it or not, is made to satisfy certain needs, although we often don't–or can't–articulate those needs. Every decision is made to function, to produce certain expected results.

Go on.

Long run effectiveness means the organization is achieving the purpose for which it exists. Short term effectiveness means that doing whatever we are doing propels us toward the satisfaction of that purpose.

For a business it's profits, right?

Yes, that's the final outcome, but don't make the same mistake I did in my book *How to Solve the Mismanagement Crisis*. The mistake is to confuse input, throughput, and output. Have you ever seen companies so preoccupied with profits that they're going bankrupt? They're losing money not *in spite* of, but *because* of their preoccupation with profits. If you are preoccupied with happiness as a goal and you wake up every morning telling yourself, "I must be happy today," you can make yourself quite miserable. The same with health. Obsession with the subject can make you a hypochondriac. Profits, like happiness, health, and democracy, are an output, not an input. Profits are like the score in a tennis match. Too many people watch the score rather than the ball when they're playing tennis. If you have a good tennis coach, he'll tell you not to think about the score when you're playing. Every volley should be like the first of the match, as if you were starting from zero. If you're preoccupied with the score, you can't play well.

It's the same with managing. I disagree with books whose exclusive focus is management *by* results. It should be management *for* results and *by* the right process. Management by results is mechanistic. It's primarily managing by output, or by the score, with a lower focus on input and throughput. No *primary* attention is given to the means of achieving the goals.

Marksmanship is a good example of paying attention to the means of achieving a goal, which is to hit the bull's-eye. To hit the bull's-eye, you must align the sights of your gun with the target. The sights are the means by which you hit the target.

What does this have to do with the means of achieving a goal?

The human eye is like a camera. It cannot focus simultaneously with the same clarity on the target, which is a hundred yards away, as on the sights, which are inches away. Most people focus on the target, on what they want to achieve. In the process of doing so they necessarily de-emphasize the sights, the means of achieving the goal. And a single hundredth-of-an-inch mistake in the sights can make all the difference in where the bullet will hit the target, or whether it will hit it at all.

There are people who believe that the goal is more important than the means, so they ignore the importance of the process by which the goal is achieved. Yet a slight misalignment in the process can defeat the desired results. You must focus on the sights and accept the relative haziness of the target. Train your mind to focus on the means, *in the direction of* the goal or the results you want to achieve.

> *That's interesting. I always think more about where I want to go than about how to get there.*

You're not the only one. Goals are exciting. Thinking about means and the values that should govern how those goals are achieved is frequently boring and complicated.

> *But what should we focus on in managing a company, if not on profits? Are you ignoring profits? Isn't the purpose of playing to win?*

First of all, it's not profit as such. If you make effective and efficient decisions, you will produce added value. Profit is one way to measure added value. It is the right measurement for some business organizations and the totally wrong one for other organizations, such as not–for–profits.

Let's look at this more closely. If you are effective, you have done something functional. You have satisfied a need. The satisfaction is manifested by the fact that people are willing to pay for it. And payment does not have to be in monetary terms. It could be measured by how long people are willing to wait in line for a free service that is available competitively. If you provided the service efficiently, you have done it at minimum cost. When people in a competitive environment are willing to pay you more than what it costs you to provide it, you have created added value. The value of satisfying the need is higher than the cost of producing that satisfaction. Thus, profit is one manifestation of value added and is the appropriate measurement for business organizations, because their purpose in society is economic.

Input ⟶	Output	
Decision roles	**Organizational Characteristics**	
- -	effectiveness ⎫	short
- -	efficiency ⎭	run
- -	effectiveness ⎫	long
- -	efficiency ⎭	run

Long and Short Term Profit = Added Value

For other organizations, the not–for–profit organizations whose purpose or function for the society is different, the added value should be measured differently. Consider a hospital. Depending on the type of hospital, the method of measuring value added will necessarily be different. For a teaching hospital, added value can be measured by the number of medical doctors it graduated while maintaining its economic viability. If it is a research hospital, it can be measured by the contributions the staff has made to professional journals.

The focus of the not–for–profit should be first on its function in society, then on the value it has to create and how to measure that value, and finally on minimizing the cost of creating that value. We should start with how to create value, how to be functional. In the long run, we should focus on how to contribute to the bigger system the organization belongs to. And that means we must focus on how to accomplish the purpose for which the organization exists.

How do I do this?

The reason an organization exists is clearest at its inception. At that time, it is established for a definite purpose. Let's illustrate it through an analogy.

Five friends get together Friday night and have some beers. As they are drinking, someone suggests they go on a hike to the nearest lake the next morning. The rest of the group enthusiastically agrees. The next day, they walk down a narrow mountain path on their way to the lake. As they are walking, they're whistling, joking, laughing, maybe even arguing with each other.

Now imagine that the group arrives at a point on this narrow path where a rock is blocking their passage. The rock is so big that none of them *alone* can lift it. What does the group have to do now?

Move that rock.

And since no one alone can lift it, they have to interrelate and decide what to do.

They may decide to move the rock, or they may decide to camp out then and there instead of trying to reach the lake, or they may go back home and have a barbecue.

First note that these five people were friends. Their friendship and sense of belonging expressed itself in a need to do something together.

First, that need was satisfied by drinking beer. Then it was satisfied by going on a hike to a lake. Then it was satisfied by working together either to lift the rock or to come up with another plan. Relating and interrelating is the ultimate purpose for our existence. There is nothing in this world that doesn't exist to serve something else by functionally interrelating to it. The pen I write with has no meaning if it does not leave a mark on paper. Breathing is useless unless the oxygen feeds my body. Nothing in itself is functional. The ability of anything to function is evaluated by how it serves its clients. The final purpose of existence of any system is (I)ntegration, the *(I)* role. The process of identifying a new need that satisfies that ultimate purpose—going on a hike rather than drinking beer—is (E)ntrepreneuring, the *(E)* role. The actual act of drinking beer, hiking to a lake, or removing the rock on the road, the act of doing whatever satisfies the purpose of the interrelationship at that moment, is (P)erforming, the *(P)* role.

Now let's assume one of the five friends had a system for removing rocks efficiently. This person had done it many times before and had developed an efficient procedure. The group will not have to do the job through trial and error. That is (A)dministering, the *(A)* role.

Could you detail these four roles for me and give some examples.

The *(P)* role focuses on *what* to do now and is derived from *why* we do *what* we do. The *(E)* role focuses on *why* we do something—the *what for* of our actions. It focuses on satisfying our long-term need. But both in the short and long run whatever we do is a call for interrelationship. Behind every problem there is a relationship that does not function, and the solution is to make the relationship functional. In personal life this need to interrelate is called the need for love. Every problem is a manifestation of a lack of love, and the solution is to experience it. The ultimate *why* we do anything, the interrelationship, is the *(I)* role. That is the ultimate and constant need, (I)ntegration. It expresses itself by different yearnings, such as to go and drink beer together, hike together, or paddle a canoe together. The process of identifying a new need that will help encourage and express that interrelationship is (E)ntrepreneuring. The act of satisfying the need is to (P)rovide a needed service.

So the (E) role is to identify a new need that expresses, encourages, and satisfies this purpose of interrelationship; and the (P) role is to

*fulfill the immediate purpose for which the organization exists,
that is, to fulfill the purpose of the interrelationship.*

Right. The problem with some large organizations is that by the time they
employ several thousand people, very few, if any, of the employees know
why they are walking or where they are walking or where the rock is.

Because they're all sitting on the rock?

Yes, and pushing each other. "You're stepping on me." "No, you're stepping on me." They are preoccupied with turf wars. They spend their time
dwelling on the liability rather than on the purpose and benefit of their
interrelationship and interdependence.

This is interesting, but where are you going with your argument?

Interrelationship, (I)ntegration, is forever and constant. It expresses itself
in different needs we wish to satisfy in the future. It is like saying that spirit
is constant and forever. It expresses itself through different bodies when we
are born, and it continues to exist when we die. And this (I)ntegration
exists as long as we serve each other for a totality that will in turn serve us.
That's the road to being alive forever through your deeds and not through
your body.
    The ultimate purpose, to be (I)ntegrated, to be functionally interde-
pendent, is constant, just as spirit is constant. An organization as a form of
functional interdependence is born in the way a body as an embodiment of
the spirit is born, when a *particular* functional interdependence is identified and a commitment is made to fulfill it.

*And what is that? How does that happen? When does a particular
expression of this constant interdependence start? When is an organization born?*

When founders of a company become inspired to start the company, they
call their banker, their parents, and anyone else they need to call. They take
out loans and set up the company. Now, what did they see before their eyes
that day they were inspired? Did they see profits?

I don't think so. When people start companies, they won't see any profits in the first few months, or maybe even years. As a matter of fact, if they closed up shop and went to work for somebody else during that time, they'd make more money.

So what did they see?

An opportunity to make profits.

Note the choice of words: an *opportunity* to make profits. That tells you that you have to focus on the opportunity, and if you exploit the opportunity correctly you will reap profits. From our previous analogy you can see that the profit is the bull's–eye and the opportunity the sights. You must focus on the opportunity, and if you do it efficiently, you will make profits. And what do you think that opportunity is?

Well, added value is created by satisfying the needs that someone is willing to pay to have satisfied. So the opportunities we are talking about are the needs in the marketplace that are currently not being satisfied well or at all, and that could be satisfied by the new company the founder is contemplating. Founders see needs they believe they can satisfy and that should be satisfied. When needs meet capabilities, an opportunity is born.

Right. An organization is born when the interdependence is realized and a commitment is made to satisfy it. The first thing to note is that the founders were conscious; they were not sleeping. They were conscious, aware, sensitive to something else beyond themselves. Out of that consciousness of interdependence, the *(I)* role, came a specific awareness of specific perceived needs that can and should be satisfied. That need could be for ice cream or a new medicine that will cure a disease. This is the *(E)* role, identifying the specific long–term need that should be satisfied. Then the founders get moving on the path towards satisfying that long–term need and in the process encounter obstacles (rocks). Removing rocks, *(P)*, is functional when it enables the founders to move closer to their long term goal, *(E)*, without ruining the grand purpose of the whole enterprise, which is to functionally (I)nterrelate.

The person who on that Friday night suggested a hike noted a new need to experientially interrelate. It could have been to a lake or to a mountain peak. He or she is sensitive to what the people aspire to. When the group comes across the rock, this person should still be sensitive to the grand need to interrelate functionally. And in light of that, he or she should lead the process of removing the rock or abandoning the hike.

But what do you mean by "interrelate functionally"?

I mean create added value. If the process of removing the rock creates tension and fighting while the purpose of the hike was to have fun together, what should he or she do?

Change the destination.

The same holds true for a marriage. What is the purpose of being married? Is it to have children or to love and be loved, in which case the children are an expression of the couple's love for one another? What about a couple that cannot have children? Should they divorce, or can they find another manifestation of love through which they can experience their purpose of being together? What if they have problems in their marriage? Those problems are "rocks" blocking their passage to the lake: issues like career decisions, what house to buy, how to spend money. How can those rocks be removed? What are the right decisions? It depends on what they are committed to or why they are together in the first place. If it is love, being right about how to remove the rock correctly and vigorously insisting on it can be quite wrong. They may move the rock, arrive at the lake, and find they destroyed the purpose of why they went to the lake in the first place.

In managing, leading, parenting, interrelating in a marriage, and interrelating in general, always ask yourself: What is the purpose of the relationship in the first place? What are you committed to first and above all? The answer, if you are conscious, is love, and if you are confused as to how love got into the conversation, relax. It will become clearer later. For the time being, ask yourself as far as you can be conscious, what are you committed to? What is the long and short-term need for which the interrelationship of your organization exists, whether that organization is you personally, your marriage, your business, or society? Next, ask yourself how you should satisfy those needs without undermining the interrelationship itself.

An organization is born when those needs cannot be satisfied by any single individual. If they could be, there would be no need for an organization whether it be a family, a business, a state, or a global society. The purpose of any organization is to satisfy its clients' needs that cannot be satisfied by an individual alone. When an organization is very young, the purpose is clearly visible, because a young organization cannot forget the clients. If it does, it goes bankrupt. The company wants the clients' repeat business, or else it may not have the cash to pay salaries.

As organizations grow older, they focus more and more on the score, on profits, on measurable output, on the lake. They forget who the clients are and what needs they must satisfy. They start to focus exclusively on profits. At that point many companies go bankrupt, not *in spite of* focusing on profits, but *because* they were focusing exclusively on profits.

But why? Why do they become more far-sighted as they get older? It's like what happens to people's vision as they age.

That is the subject of another book of mine, *Corporate Lifecycles*. Look there if you're interested.

To make effective decisions in the short and long run, you must satisfy the immediate reasons for your actions and satisfy the long-term needs for why you do what you do. And it has to be done within the reason of your existence. That reason is to functionally interrelate and that means, as will become clearer later, to love and be loved. You do that by satisfying your clients' needs. Simply stated, analyze your clients. Identify what it is that they need and expect from you that you can and should provide. Then go and do it.

I see. I should analyze my customers!

No. I purposely used the word *clients*, not *customers*. Many people confuse the two.

What's the difference?

Every organizational entity has clients. These are the individuals or groups of individuals for which the entity was established in order to satisfy their needs. Every organizational unit, even if it does not deal with customers, has clients. Paying clients are called customers. For the sales department, their clients are the...

Customers.

Right. They are the outside–paying clients. And where are the clients of the accounting department?

Inside the organization.

You should do with the inside what you do with the outside. With customers you do marketing research, don't you? You ask them, "What do you want? Are you satisfied?" Well, do the same thing with internal clients. Research their needs. You'll learn a lot, just as companies learn when they (P)erform marketing research. Sometimes companies learn that what the customers don't want is being provided amply, while what the customers do want is not provided at all. The same holds true for internal clients.

If you want to be effective in the short term, the first step you must take in decision making is to find out who your present clients are and what their present needs are. You do that by being aware of interrelationships and interdependencies, by having a sense of belonging to a larger scheme of things. That is the *(I)* role. Identifying the clients' long–term needs that call out to be satisfied is the *(E)* role. We will discuss these roles in detail later. For now, these roles function to identify *for whom* the organization exists and *why* it exists. The immediate action itself, the *what* we are doing—producing shoes or removing the rock—is the *(P)* role, (P)erforming the task, (P)roviding for the satisfaction of the need for which the interrelationships exist.

Perhaps this chart will help you see this more clearly.

Purpose of Decision Making   **Role**

For Whom, Who are the clients, *Why* we exist .... *(I)*

What are their needs,

    i.e., *Why* do we do anything .... *(E)*

What we do to satisfy those needs .... *(P)*

How do we satisfy those needs

    repetitively with minimum energy .... *(A)*

How do you measure and validate what you are performing, let's say, the (P) role?

Short–term effectiveness can be measured by repeat business. If the clients are not coming back, apparently you're not satisfying their needs. This applies to a society too, you know! Isn't it interesting that they don't check your passport going *out* of the United States, only coming in? In the Soviet Union, until recently, they had guards with machine guns keeping people *in*. Which people's needs are being satisfied more? The same is true for a marriage!

What if the internal clients have no choice? If they are not allowed to have their needs satisfied by outside people?

Some clients have to come back because you have a monopoly over what they need. At best, they will complain. The worst is when you hear no complaints. It seems good because you hear nothing, but apathy is one step away from death. In these cases, you have an even bigger responsibility to take the initiative and find out if clients are coming back because you are satisfying their needs or because they have to come back. It's a difficult assignment to self–start, because you could easily avoid doing it. There is no external pressure to do it. That is also why in a marriage we have to pay special attention to the needs of our spouse, of what he or she expects from the marriage. We should not take our spouse for granted simply because, supposedly, he or she doesn't have a choice to go outside the marriage to satisfy his or her needs.

You want to be effective in the short term? Identify the clients, the *(I)* role, then their needs, the *(E)* role, and satisfy those needs, the *(P)* role, and your clients will return to you.

Could you repeat that, please?

The *(I)* role tells you who the clients are, the *(E)* role what their long–term needs are. To perform the *(P)* role, you have to go and remove whatever "rocks" are blocking you from satisfying the need for which you are interrelating without destroying the ability of the relationship to function in the process. I disagree with books that say "a manager is a manager is a manager. If you are a manager, you can manage anything." This is wrong—unless you add three more words: *after some time.*

What does that mean?

When you change jobs, either within a company or when you leave for another company, you come across a new organization, a new set of clients. No two identical organizations exist, just as no two identical people exist. They may be similar, but never identical. No two identical branches of the same bank exist. They're on different corners, have different parking problems, and attract different customers from different industries.

So what do I have to do?

You have to study the new rock. And what should you focus on? The normal tendency of people is to focus on what? On similarities or on differences?

People usually focus on similarities. They try to find out whether they recognize anything. They find comfort when they recognize a task they already know. You're wincing. Is this a typical mistake?

You have to look for the differences too. Only then can you design a custom made strategy to satisfy the specific needs of that moment. When you meet a new love in your life, do you look for similarities and say, "You remind me of an old flame," or do you look for what is unique in this new person?

Better the latter obviously.

The same is true in managing. You should ask, "How is this 'rock' different from any other rock I know?" To be effective, good managers, whether supervisors, department managers, parents, or sociopolitical leaders, should know the *unique* needs of their clients at that moment and then be skillful with their unique capabilities to satisfy those needs.

You're saying that to manage is to decide and implement. In order to decide, four roles need to be performed. The first one, the (P) role, will make the organization effective in the short run. It requires that we satisfy the immediate needs of the client for whom the system exists and do what it takes to satisfy those needs. Right?

Right, and for that you need what psychologists call achievement motivation. You must want to accomplish things. If you know the client's needs and how to satisfy them, but lack achievement motivation, you could be a good staff person. You could assist managers to manage, write memos, and make recommendations. On the other hand, if you have the motivation to achieve, but don't know what must be accomplished or how, you are dangerous. You're an unguided missile. This combination of qualities is often seen in eager young executives. They are eager but lack knowledge or experience.

In government we have examples of nonelected technocrats who are given power and are eager to use it. The politicians who need things done use these people, but if these technocrats have little political experience and judgment, they overuse their power and endanger the political survival of their bosses.

Good managers, to be functional and make effective decisions, must be knowledgeable achievers, not just knowledgeable, and not just achievers.

That covers how to be effective in the short run: (P)! (P)! (P)! First identify the clients (I), second, identify the needs you are uniquely qualified to satisfy (E), and third, go and do it, (P). I'm still unclear about those roles, but I trust it will become clearer in future conversations.

Yes, it will. We will definitely clarify these roles many more times. This is enough for today. Let's take a swim, rest and come back some other time.

Thank you.

Conversation 3

Efficiency and Effectiveness

Now, where did we leave off?

> *We discussed securing short–term effectiveness by satisfying imme-*
> *diate client needs. Being effective in the short run is necessary for a*
> *good decision. And making good decisions is half of managing*
> *well.*

Why do we have to make decisions?

> *Because there are problems, and there are problems because there*
> *is change. We diagrammed it like this:*

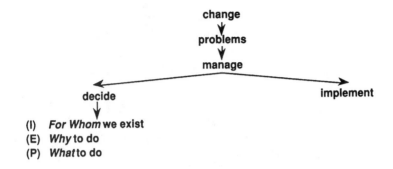

The *(P)* role makes the organization effective in the short run, because it satisfies the present needs of the present clients.

What about efficiency?

Short–term *efficiency* is also necessary. For that you need to perform another role. I call it the *(A)* role, to (A)dminister.

To be efficient you need to systematize an organization, make its processes routine. The right things must be done at the right time, in the right order, at the right intensity, and in the right sequence. You must do *things right*, rather than just do the *right things*.

You have to find the most efficient way of doing things. Instead of re-inventing the wheel every time you need to wheel something around, you design the best way to produce wheels by making the process routine. Systematization makes you efficient. It requires attention to detail, thoroughness, and a good memory. It requires not that you work harder, but that you be more disciplined.

Give me an example.

When you're hungry, you eat. Right?

Right.

Your decision to eat something is effective if it satisfies your hunger. That's *(P)*.

Now, if you systematize your eating habits with a diet, then your decision about the proper diet makes you efficient. You don't have to spend time thinking about whether to eat something or not. In making your diet decision, you are performing the *(A)* role.

> *That makes sense. A decision should produce effectiveness and efficiency. Can I be effective and not efficient?*

Good question. Let's look at how you play tennis. Hitting the ball over the net into the opponent's court proves that your decision to hit the ball was effective. However, in order to be efficient, what do you have to do? You must systematize your volley. You have to learn how to hold your racquet and move your body correctly. The coach trains you and gives you a system, by sending you the ball in the same direction over and over. This helps you develop the correct movement and swing so that you will hit the ball with maximum impact and minimum expenditure of energy.

Let's go over this again. Hitting the ball into the opponent's court makes you...

> *Effective.*

Hitting it *right* makes you...

> *Efficient.*

You could be effective and not efficient. You could hit the ball in something other than the most efficient way. You might hit the ball over the net, but if you expend more energy than necessary, you'll tire sooner.

> *How about being efficient and not effective?*

This is more difficult to recognize. In tennis, you learn in your repetitive training to hit the ball with a certain swing. When you do that perfectly, you are efficient. In order to maintain that efficiency, you may request that your opponent hit the ball in a way that you can hit it back most efficiently. You don't want to chase the ball and be forced to return it in a way that is not efficient.

> *But what does this mean in organizational terms?*

The condition occurs in many bureaucracies. They're organized to be so efficient that they begin saying, "This would be a wonderful business to run if it were not for the clients' changing demands." The ball, or the clients' needs, is not coming the way the bureaucracy is organized to handle it most efficiently.

And bureaucracies have difficulty dealing with that.

You bet. To be more effective they might have to be less efficient. Efficiency can be detrimental to effectiveness.

Is that why when a company is young, it's effective, but not very efficient? Then as it grows older, it's efficient but not effective?

Yes! To be in the Prime of your organizational lifecycle is to be effective and efficient, and that takes effort. It is not automatically forthcoming.

But if efficiency is up, then profits are up; and if profits are up then added value is up, and that's what we want in the business world, right?

Yes, but notice how the added value is computed. It is value beyond cost. When you generate profits exclusively through efficiency, profits will go up only by cutting costs. As you continually shrink costs, however, what else might go down? If you cut costs to the point that you can't satisfy your clients' needs, effectiveness will drop and sales will go down. There is a lag, however, between the time when the client's needs are not satisfied and when clients find someone else's business to patronize. It takes time to build their satisfaction (sales), and it also takes time to lose their loyalty. Sales decrease more slowly than the cuts in expenses. This time lag between when you cut costs and when you see sales decline can make your company look profitable while it is actually going bankrupt. You will be profitable in the short run, but eventually the deterioration in your sales will catch up. You'll have no clients left to milk.

I understand. We need to be both effective and efficient. We can add it to the diagram.

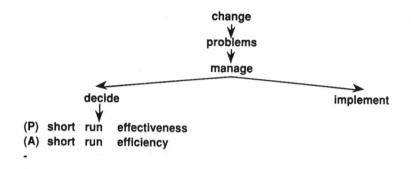

(P) short run   effectiveness
(A) short run   efficiency
-
-

*Now, tell me what do we need for long–run effectiveness? I under-
stand that in order to be effective and efficient in the short run, I
need to (P)erform a needed service, and (A)dminister it. Now for
effectiveness in the long run?*

Long–Run Effectiveness
Long–run effectiveness means that your present decision will satisfy future
client needs. What we want is a decision that produces effectiveness in the
long run, one that can predict and satisfy new needs we believe will emerge.
For that, a decision needs to make the organization proactive.

Give me an example.

Back to the beer–drinking party. Sitting there watching the camaraderie,
the creatively conscious individual identified the group members' need to
relate to each other in a way that beer drinking alone did not satisfy. So this
leader suggested they go for a hike to a lake so they could go canoeing. So
the leader suggested, "Let's go canoeing tomorrow." The leader enabled a
decision to be made that night that would satisfy the needs of tomorrow.

*Wait a minute. The need to hike to a lake and go canoeing oc-
curred that night. That's why they agreed to go for a hike. Right? So
why do you say the (E) role is to identify the needs of tomorrow
today?*

What happens if the next day they wake up and feel they really don't want
to go hiking and canoeing? The decision of the previous evening might

turn sour. The test of *(E)* is not in when you are deciding but in when you are achieving. *(E)* identifies the needs of tomorrow, which *(P)* validates by actually satisfying those needs.

Give me another example.

Let's assume you have decided to build a factory *today* that will produce gadgets you predict will be needed *next year*. When next year arrives, your prediction proves to be true and the demand is there. Your decision to build a factory *today* will make you effective *tomorrow*.

Let's go back to the tennis analogy. As you hit the ball, what else do you have to do? You must think about where your opponent's next shot will land. You may have to run to the net, to the middle of the court, or to the baseline in order to meet that next ball. This process of *positioning* yourself for future needs is called being *proactive*.

A *proactive* approach will make you effective in the long run. If you're in the right place when the next ball arrives, you will be ready to hit it again. What makes you effective in the long run is your *positioning now*, for which we need the *(E)* role.

The *(P)* role satisfies present client needs. The *(E)* role identifies future needs and positions the organization to deal with them. *(E)* precedes *(P)*. First you identify the clients' needs; then you go and satisfy those needs. First you predict where the ball is going to land; then you go there and hit it back over the net.

So (E)ntrepreneuring means to position myself for the future by doing something about it today. That way, when tomorrow comes, I'll be ready to deal with it.

Yes, and I'm not talking about marketing or merchandising. I'm talking about *positioning* yourself to meet future needs. Are you getting ready with a new product? Are you getting ready with new distribution channels? Are you equipping yourself with a new technology so that you'll be able to satisfy the needs you predict? As you sit and drink beer, you think about future needs the present beer drinking does not satisfy and you come to a decision that night that will satisfy those future needs.

You have to adapt to a changing environment.

What does adapting mean to you? Is it proactive or reactive?

Reactive.

Right. The people who *adapt* to a changing environment are the ones who wait until the ball lands in the court. Once they know where it has landed, they *adapt*, they react, to it. But by then it might be too late. Adapting is *(P)*. For (E)ntrepreneuring and positioning, you must be proactive, not reactive.

In order to be proactive, you need two things. First you have to imagine what the future will look like. You have to build scenarios of future client needs, the competition, the environment, and anything else that might affect the organization. You have to be creative and imagine what is going to happen.

What do you mean by "creative"?

The future is foggy. Creative people can see through that fog. You may not have all the information, and the validity of what you do have changes with time. Indistinct visions appear, then disappear. You have to assemble the available information then fill in the gaps by using your imagination. That's creativity: filling informational gaps to create a whole picture.

But it takes more than being creative to be proactive. After you predict where the next ball is going to land, what is the second thing you must do?

You have to actually make your move on the court.

Yes, you have to take a risk. You must run to a spot on the court and position yourself for the next ball. And since the ball may not land where you predicted, you're taking a risk.

$$(E)\text{ntrepreneuring} = f \left\{ \begin{array}{l} 1.\ \text{creativity} \\ 2.\ \text{risk taking} \end{array} \right\}$$

Some people are creative but not risk–takers. They're not (E)ntrepreneuring or proactive. Usually you find such people in the consulting or business teaching professions. They're creative. They can forsee the future. But they are unwilling to take the risk and act upon what they see. Gamblers, on the other hand, are risk–takers, but are not creative. They don't design the game. The ideal balance for the *(E)* role in a manager is someone who can imagine the future and then take the risks to position the organization to deal with that future.

And if you are proactive you will be effective in the long run?

Yes, because as the expected needs arise, you will be ready to respond.

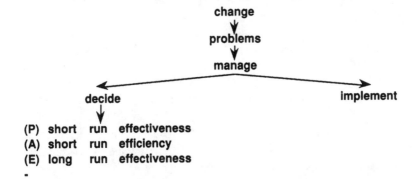

Now I am ready to learn about the fourth role: how to become efficient in the long run.

This is the most difficult role to explain.

I'm ready! I assume we will later have exercises so I can really understand these roles.

Yes, we will.

That sounds good to me.

Long–Term Efficiency

In order to be efficient in the long run, one must (I)ntegrate, which means *to transform the consciousness of the organization—its personality, value systems, behavior pattern, and philosophy—from mechanistic to organic.* You (I)ntegrate, for instance, when you teach people to play team sports. All the participants share emotionally, socially, and sometimes economically from winning. It is not a star system, but an ensemble. When building a team, you build the teammates' support for each other so they will benefit or lose as a team rather than as individuals.

Now let's explain each of the words in our definition above. Let's start with the word *organization.* If I were to ask you, "How many people are in your organization?" where would you look for the answer?

I would look in the personnel files or at the organization chart.

Exactly, and those are the wrong places to look. As a manager, in order to find out who the people are that you're supposed to (I)ntegrate, motivate, and manage, don't look at your organization chart.

But aren't the people who report to me the ones I have to manage?

I have never met a manager who claimed, "All the people I need to carry out my responsibilities report to me." Never! The managers I know always claim the opposite. Their usual complaint is that they have difficulty carrying out their responsibilities because people critical to the tasks do not report to them. Sam Armacost, who was president of Bank of America, had the best response to the situation: "You don't need to own a highway in order to drive on it. You need only a token to get on it."

But surely the presidents of companies have everyone they need reporting to them.

Really? The unions do not report to the company president. Neither do the bankers, the stockholders, the clients, or the competitors. From below it looks as if presidents have everything under control, but they often only act that way to demonstrate authority. Upon closer inspection, one might find they are lonely at the top and frequently feel powerless to carry out their responsibility.

Yes, I guess we're all lonely and vulnerable, except some admit it and some don't.

Some are paid more not to admit it.

Then where should I, as a manager or leader, look to find the organization I am supposed to manage?

Start with looking at the clients for whom the organization exists. That's your *(I)* role. That means being conscious of your responsibility to others. No one exists for oneself only.

Really? I know people who are totally self–centered and couldn't care less about anyone else.

The moment you exist exclusively for yourself, you become a cancer. Cancerous cells use energy for non–functional purposes. They serve nothing and no one but themselves. Some people are cancerous entities in an organization, and some organizations are cancerous entities in a society. The world is created so that everything exists to support something else in a functioning totality, which then functions to serve its components. That is the ecological balance we are all so preoccupied with nowadays.

So beginning any organization, society, or community means being conscious of the interdependence. It is this spiritual consciousness of Who am I? which is always answered with the question, For Whom and For What am I?

We could modify Descartes' statement, "I think, therefore I am," to "I serve, therefore I am." Rabbi Abraham Heschel once said, "If I am not for myself, who will be for me? And if I am only for myself, then who am I?"

There is no healthy organization without a sense of common destiny linking it to a larger scheme. There must be a consciousness of interdependence, whether the organization is a nation, a business, a marriage, or an individual.

After you identify for whom the organization exists (the clients), you should identify the people whose cooperation you need in order to satisfy the needs of those clients. Let's go back to the group of friends who are trying to remove the rock blocking their path. Assume that in order to remove the rock to reach the lake for canoeing you need the assistance of park rangers. The rangers will do it because they are paid to help hikers, but they do not organizationally report to you. Maybe you need other hikers to help lift the rock, and they don't get paid at all to help you. But do you need them? Yes, you do. And since your whole group needs them in order to achieve your goal, the other hikers and park rangers are all members of your organization who need to be coordinated, motivated and, in a word, managed.

As far as your organizational responsibility is concerned, you should look at the "rock" you are responsible for lifting. Some of the people you need to help you lift the rock work for you directly. They're on your payroll. They're the employees on your organizational chart. Some people necessary to lift the rock do not work directly for you. They are in other departments. Maybe they're your peers. Maybe they're your superiors. Maybe they're even outside the organization. The people you are supposed to manage are all those people you need to lift the rock and all those who get satisfaction from moving that rock.

By the way, you can look beyond the rock, depending on your consciousness. The organization you feel responsible to and for might include not only those people needed to move the rock, but all those needed to get to the lake, and if you raise your eyes higher, you will realize that the rock is irrelevant and so is the lake. They all change over time. What is constant is the human race, whose needs change whether it is a rock or a lake. And if you continue looking up, you will realize that you are relating functionally, serving and being served by the human race, by plants, animals, rocks...practically anything that surrounds you. You will feel responsible to serve a totality for that totality to serve you.

How do I operationally do this— tomorrow morning?

Look at the *(PAEI)* codes. Start by asking, "Who are my clients?" For *whom* do I exist? This is the first group of people you need to know of—the first part of your *(I)* role. Next, identify the needs of those clients. That's your *(E)* role. The next question should be, *What* specifically should the organization do and *how* does it go about doing it? Those are your *(P)* and *(A)* roles. *What* needs to be done *(P)*, and *how* it needs to be done *(A)*, will then lead you to analyze *who* should do it, which is the second part of your *(I)* role. "*Who* do I need in order to satisfy my clients' needs?" Do I also need rangers, other hikers, and so on? That's the organization that you need to manage.

Then ask, "What do the people needed for lifting the rock or arriving at the lake want from the organization?" What is in it for them if they cooperate? To some, the organization pays a salary. To others, it pays no salary but someone has to take them to dinner and massage their egos. Others are paid commissions. How they get paid is irrelevant, as long as it is ethical and legal. Your job is to find out how the organization should reward them so that they cooperate in satisfying the needs of your clients.

The people you need to satisfy the clients' needs are called stakeholders, whether they are paid a salary or rewarded in some other way. Like the clients, they have a self–interest. Employees, salaried or otherwise, and stockholders, for instance, are stakeholders. Both groups have something at stake: the satisfaction of their needs is based upon how the organization performs. How about management? They also have needs.

That's why they are in the organization. So they're stakeholders as well. How about the community in which the organization is located? Does it have something at stake? You bet. You must make all stakeholders realize that if they cooperate, their own needs will be satisfied. You have to create a win–win climate in which money and salary are not the only means of exchange. You have to synchronize the needs of the clients with the needs of the stakeholders. When the stakeholders recognize that their needs are satisfied by satisfying client needs, that they need each other to satisfy each other's needs, the organization is (I)ntegrated. When everyone is (I)ntegrated, then no one is indispensable, and the organization is going to be efficient in the long run.

A manager has to make people cooperate. I've got it. But how?

I'll cover this subject in more detail later. The bottom line is that you should focus on self–interest and common interest. When self–interest equals common interest you have succeeded in (I)ntegrating.

Mechanistic Versus Organic Consciousness

What about the words mechanistic and organic? You used them in your definition of (I)ntegration. What do they mean?

Imagine a chair with four legs standing in the middle of the room. Why is it called a chair? Why don't we call it a cow?

Well if you could milk it, you could call it a cow.

Yes! For the purposes of our discussion, we can say that what something is, is what it does. If it does not perform the function, then it is not the object. If you tell me the function, I can tell you the name of the object.

If you have a piano that is not being played, it's not a piano. It's a piece of furniture. If you have a chair you cannot sit on, it is not a chair. It could be a piece of Memphis art. If I show you a hammer and ask, "What is this?" you know enough to say, "I don't know what it is until you tell me what you do with it. If you pound nails with it, then it's a hammer. If you use it to harm someone, it's a weapon. If you collect different types of hammers from around the world to hang in your garage, then it's a decoration."

We don't know what something is until we know its function, what need it satisfies. You cannot say you are a father if you have never done anything to satisfy your child's needs. You might be a biological father, but if you're not fulfilling the child's social, economic, and emotional needs, you're not a parenting father. You are what you do, and what you do has functional meaning through the needs you satisfy.

Now let's go back to the chair. It's a chair because we can sit on it. It fulfills the function of providing a place to sit. Now, what will happen if a leg breaks off?

We no longer have a functioning chair. We have a broken chair. We cannot sit on it.

And the question is, why doesn't one of the remaining legs move to the center of the chair, creating a tripod, so that the chair can continue to function? The answer is obvious: the chair is mechanistic. It's like a machine. In order for the chair to fulfill its role, someone from the *outside* has to fix it. This chair is dependent on external intervention to function. There is no internal interdependence between the parts of a chair. A multimillion dollar spaceship can explode in flight and kill seven people because an O-ring does not function. No other part can take the place of that O-ring. This is called mechanistic consciousness.

Now let's look at organic consciousness. Look at your hand. It's a hand because you can grasp objects: it functions as a hand. What would happen if you broke or lost one of the fingers? Would you still have a hand?

Yes. It wouldn't be as good, but I would still have a hand.

Why?

Because the other four fingers would compensate. The hand would continue to function.

Exactly. What makes a hand a hand is not just the physical attributes of the five fingers. It's that each of the five fingers "thinks" like a hand. If each leg on the chair thought, *I'm a leg and part of a chair*, then each leg would support its function. The chair would have an organic instead of a mechanistic consciousness.

Let's look at humans. Why do our legs run when our eyes see danger? Because it is as if through organic consciousness all our body parts recognize the benefits and liabilities of their interdependence and work to protect the whole. In a mechanistic consciousness each part is conscious only of itself. There is no internal sense of interdependence. In an organization with a mechanistic consciousness, production people worry only about production, and sales people worry only about sales. And who worries about whether the totality functions? Outsiders have to worry about the totality and have to intervene because none of the individuals involved worry about it. That intervention is often undertaken by management. In such an organization, employees view and oppose management as if it were an outsider.

An extreme case is when management also worries only about its own interests, and not about the totality it manages. In that case, the external intervention is provided by consultants, by the government, or by no one, in which case the organization dis(I)ntegrates and might go bankrupt.

This discussion reminds me of a story: Three people are laying bricks. If you ask the first person, "What are you doing?" he might answer, "I'm laying bricks." The second person might respond, "I'm building a wall." The third person might answer, "We are building a temple where we are going to worship the Lord together."

Only the third person understands the purpose of the whole enterprise and recognizes the benefits to be shared from each person's function. Through prayer, in whichever form it is done, a person becomes (I)ntegrated with the Lord. And that (I)ntegration, in order to be fully realized, has to be *within* oneself, *between* oneself and others, and *outside* of the immediate circle into the larger scheme to which one belongs. We become aware of God when we become conscious that everything and everybody belongs to one large interrelated system. When we become conscious of that, we realize we are one, although we have different forms, shapes, and textures. The difference is necessary for the functioning of the total. Through differences we serve each other in a totality in order for the totality to serve us. And that totality has consciousness too, a total absolute and everlasting one. That's God to me.

In the chair example, if every leg understood and supported the benefits of being part of a sitting system, then the chair would have an organic consciousness. It wouldn't be a broken chair, because each part would compensate for the system's vulnerability and do its best to make the system function. The chair would be less dependent on any one of its parts. It would work like a hand.

I think I understand. To be efficient in the long run, an organization should act like a hand in which no finger is indispensable. In an organization, teamwork should be such that each person supports the other, so that no one is indispensable.

Right. Ask yourself, What is my managerial responsibility? What is my rock? Who are the clients and what are their needs? Then ask, Who are the stakeholders I need to help lift the rock, and how do I foster the necessary interdependence between stakeholders and clients? How do I get people to realize that we need each other? For instance, do we have a common mission? Do we have a reward system that nurtures cooperation? If people share a vision and have a reward system that nurtures the pursuit and achievement of that mission cooperatively, then it is likely no one will be indispensable. People will back each other up and not wait for an outsider to fix their problems. If the answer is that the organization does not have a culture and a system that fosters interdependence, you should create that environment and (I)ntegrate the clients and stakeholders. When clients get satisfied by satisfied stakeholders, you have a system in which no one is indispensable.

Let's look at a summary of the roles.

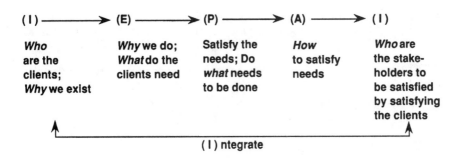

When no one is indispensable, the organization is efficient in the long run.

And now what?

The organization does not become effective and efficient in the short and long run by itself. Someone needs to make *(PAEI)* decisions that will then make the *(PAEI)* organization produce *(PAEI)* results. These results produce short and long–term value added, which certain types of organizations measure by profits. Whose role is it to see that *(PAEI)* decisions are made? That is the role of leadership, management, parenting, or government.

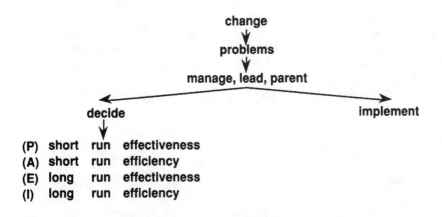

I'm looking forward to the exercises, because this was really confusing!

We will have many exercises. Now let's take a break. Tomorrow, in our next conversation, we'll start analyzing what happens when any one of these roles—(P)erforming a needed service, (A)dministering, (E)ntrepreneuring, or (I)ntegrating—is missing. We will learn how to diagnose leaders or managers and companies. If we see something is not working, we will be able to identify what's missing. If we know why it is happening, we will know what to do about it!

Summary

Let me summarize to see if I understand the material. This was very complicated, to say the least. I hope it will become clearer later.

Yes, it will become clearer through lots of discussions and examples. Trust me. Hang in there!

Okay. To manage change a decision has to be made and implemented. What are good decisions?
   Good decisions make the organization effective and efficient in the short and the long run. They make the organization functional, systematized, proactive, and organic in consciousness.

input	throughput	output
Decision Roles:	**Make Organizations:**	**To be:**
(P)rovide needed service	functional	effective short run
(A)dminister	systematized	efficient short run
(E)ntrepeneur	proactive	effective long run
(I)ntegrate	organic	efficient long run

Short and long term added value = Profits (for instance)

To be effective in the short run, the organization has to (P)rovide for the clients' needs. The (P) role can be measured by repeat sales.
   Efficiency in the short run means using the least amount of resources, including managerial time, to accomplish something. For that the organization needs to be (A)dministered, systematized, and organized. In order to do that, the organization needs discipline.

For effectiveness in the long run, the organization has to be (E)ntrepreneurial, to proact. It has to imagine the future clients' needs and position itself to be able to satisfy those needs. In order to do that, it has to be creative and willing to take risks.

For efficiency in the long run, the organization needs to be (I)ntegrated by creating a climate of cooperation between and among all stakeholders to satisfy the needs of the clients. If all stakeholders cooperate and no one is indispensable, the organization can be efficient in the long run. For that the organization has to identify and be sensitive to the needs of all the stakeholders and clients, and design a system, a climate that mutually satisfies those needs.

Good summary!

Thank you. This was interesting, although heavy. You covered a lot of material. Let me think about it for awhile.

Okay, but from now on, we won't have to cover as much theory. Instead we can focus on applications.

Sounds great. Let's resume tomorrow.

Conversation 4

The Incompatibility of Roles

I've been thinking a lot about our last conversation. Let's summarize it again.

Go ahead!

In order to manage the problems caused by change, we need to make good decisions and implement them efficiently. How well we manage is a function of the quality of the decisions we make and the amount of energy we have to spend in order to implement those decisions.

To make quality decisions, we must focus on the services that need to be (P)erformed in order to satisfy the reason for which the organization exists. This is the (P) role. It makes the organization effective only in the short run, because needed services change with time. We must also perform the (A) role, to (A)dminister, ensuring that the right things are done at the right time. This process makes the organization efficient in the short run. The (E) role, (E)ntrepreneuring, makes the organization proactive by positioning it to deal with future clients' needs. This role makes the organi-

*zation effective in the long run. The last role is the need to (I)ntegrate.
This role transforms the organization's culture from mechanistic,
where all stakeholders, including clients, feel isolated, to organic,
where people share their sense of interdependence because of mutual interests and values.*

*We need all four (PAEI) roles, which are like four "vitamins."
Anytime one of these vitamins is missing, a certain predictable
organizational disease will occur. Depending on which decision-
making role is missing, the organization could be ineffective or
inefficient in the short and/or long run. And that's what we are
going to discuss today, right?*

Right.

*I cannot remember whether we discussed the two questions I am
supposed to ask to predict the quality of the decisions an organization is going to make.*

We will discuss those questions soon. We have not done that yet. First, we
have to look at the managerial "diseases" the organization will suffer
when one of these roles is missing.

We'll start by making certain you fully understand the four roles.
You must know the *(P)*, *(A)*, *(E)* and *(I)* roles very well before we start
diagnosing systems, whether we look at people, organizations or societies.
Try to answer a few questions.

Okay.

I have two sons, Topaz and Shoham, who are fifteen months apart. Once
when they were very young, they were playing in their room while I was
reading the Sunday paper. After a while, there was a commotion and I
heard them yelling, "Daaaadeeee!" They were fighting over a xylophone. In
my family all the toys are shared, and on this day they both wanted the
xylophone.

The first question is, if they're calling for Daddy to come and solve
their problem, is their interdependence mechanistic or organic?

*Mechanistic. They are not resolving their own problem; they expect
somebody from the outside to step in.*

Right! Now what would the *(P)* solution be?

To take the xylophone away.

Stop! How should you go about finding the *(P)* solution?

After you identify the clients and identify their needs, you should analyze how to satisfy those needs and then go and do it. That is the (P) role—(P)erforming a needed service or (P)roducing desired results. It makes a decision effective.

Right! However, if you took the xylophone away, who was the client whose needs you were satisfying?

Mine, I guess. I wanted some peace and quiet.

Right. And this is a typical mistake. Many times in solving a problem, managers satisfy their own needs, not the clients' needs. So try again! What is the *(P)* solution?

Buy them another xylophone.

That may be the right solution, depending on what you assume the children's needs are. If their true need is to play the xylophone, then the solution to buy another one is a good decision. But do you believe the two toddlers are fighting over a xylophone because they really want to play Chopin?

They might be fighting because they want to make noise.

Then the solution is to give them some pots and pans from the kitchen to bang on and make noise.

Maybe they're fighting because of sibling rivalry.

Then they'll fight over the pots and pans too, because they need to fight until someone yields. The solution to the sibling rivalry could be to let them fight it out, and, unless it gets out of hand, leave them alone. If they're fighting because you're reading the newspaper and they want your attention, then they will fight until you give them your attention.

Please hear what I'm saying. The *(P)* solution is not easily identifiable, because it is derived from *(I)* and *(E)*. First of all, you have to identify who the clients are, the *(I)* role. Then you have to assume what their real needs are, the *(E)* role. Then through trial and error, you try alternative solutions until the clients are satisfied. This is the *(P)* role.

It's like selling dog food. You don't know if it's good until the dog eats it. The dog does not speak; it votes with its behavior. The same is true of humans. Don't just listen to what they say, watch what they do. Are they buying? The best proof that there is value in what you are providing is if they actually buy it. Never assume what the needs *should* be and then get upset when clients don't have those needs. Don't patronize your clients. Start by assuming what the needs are and then try to satisfy those needs until you succeed.

> *So we haven't found the (P) solution to the xylophone problem until the kids are quiet and doing something that satisfies their needs as expressed in their struggle for the xylophone.*

Right! My kids are not fighting for the xylophone. They are fighting to satisfy certain needs that the xylophone represents. The need could be to make noise, to express their sibling rivalry, to get the parent's attention, or maybe to fulfill an aesthetic need to play music.

People do not buy a product. They buy need satisfaction, and to make a *(P)* decision means to make a decision that satisfies the client's immediate needs.

> *How about (A)?*

The *(A)* role makes an organization efficient. Tell me what the *(A)* solution to the problem between my kids could be.

> *Have some law and order.*

Right, but how?

> *Well, we know the (A) role is to make the organization efficient. That means systematizing our decisions so we do not have to reinvent the wheel. In an (A) decision, we should have the same solution for the same problem. That makes us efficient. So, the (A)*

solution would be to say that one brother gets the xylophone for ten minutes, then the other one gets it for the next ten minutes, and we toss a coin to see who gets the xylophone first. We apply a family rule we can apply in all similar cases.

But what happens then? When you apply that solution, ten minutes to each child or whatever the rules of the family dictate, who is the client now?

The family, not the individual child or any other member of the family. I get it. The family is the client, and this solution ignores the children's particular needs.

And that's what happens in many organizations. When an organization is young, it looks for the *(P)* solution, ignoring *(A)*. It satisfies the clients and because of that, its sales grow bigger and bigger. And the organization gets messier and messier, until it hits a crisis. Then management says, "We need some order here." The *organization* itself emerges as a needy client. So, the company hires a professional (A)dministrator to organize the place. This person sets up budgets, information systems, organizational charts, and incentive programs. The old–timers might get upset, because the professional manager is not selling, not serving the customers. Instead, the (A)dministrator focuses on the stakeholders as the clients. In other words, first the organization develops its capability to satisfy its customers, then its focus shifts to satisfy its stakeholders. Then it (I)ntegrates both into a working totality. When this happens, the organization is in the Prime of its lifecycle. For more on this, see my book *Corporate Lifecycles.*

If the switch in focus from customers to internal stakeholders is abrupt, it can create antagonism within the organization, because the professional manager's focus could be different from what the rest of the organization is used to. The longtime employees resist, and often the professional manager is fired for doing the job he was hired to do in the first place. "He just sits in his office and works on his computer all day," they complain. "He never sells anything!" Note that in attempting the *(A)* solution, your client has changed. That tells you that the roles are interdependent. We will talk more about that later.

How about the third role? What is the (E)ntrepreneurial answer?

Would you like to try again?

> *Let me see. In order to be (E)ntrepreneurial, I have to be proactive*
> *by positioning myself for the next need. So what do I have to do? I*
> *have to find a stronger need than the one the children are fighting*
> *over. I'll say, "Let's go to the movies." I bet they'll stop bickering*
> *immediately and get ready to go.*

That's what businesses often do. When they see that sales are going down,
that client needs are not being satisfied and they can't reverse the situation,
one solution is to identify and satisfy a newer, stronger client need.

> *What about the (I) solution?*

Why don't you try again? You're doing fine.

> *My guess is to tell them to play together.*

The moment you *tell* them the solution, you are intervening, you are coming from the outside. Is that mechanistic or organic?

> *Mechanistic.*

That's why telling them to play together can be an *(A)* solution, not an *(I)*
solution.

> *What do you suggest?*

The *(I)* solution is the most difficult to design. You should not step in and
order the kids to play together, because you would reinforce their mechanistic consciousness. They would continually rely on you to resolve their
problems. In the *(I)* role, the task of management, leadership, or parenting
is, as Ralph Ablon, CEO of Ogden Corporation said, "to create an environment in which the most desirable thing will most probably happen."

> *Give me an example. How do you do that?*

In the case of the xylophone, here's what I did. I said, "How dare you two
fight? Brothers should not fight. I will not be here forever to solve the

problems between you two. Who will substitute for me after I'm gone? Lawyers and judges? The punishment for fighting is that you must give me the xylophone. Neither of you will have it. Now go to your room and don't come out until *you* have solved the problem."

You ignored them. You let them do it.

No. Ignoring them would mean not being conscious of my clients, which in the case of being a parent, are the children. I did not ignore them. I created a situation in which they had to satisfy their need by themselves, not by relying on me. A parent can't make a child be anything. A parent should create an environment in which a child can *become* the best he can be.

I see. You created an environment in which the most desirable thing would most probably happen. But is that the most desirable solution? Didn't they cry and resent the fact that you refused to solve their problem?

Sure they resented it, but that's the price they have to pay to develop their relationship. How long do you think it took for them to come out of their room?

Probably thirty seconds.

How long would it have taken them if I had said, "Take the xylophone, go to your room, and solve the problem?"

A lot longer!

Why?

Because the (P) and (I) roles are incompatible. I can see that. It's very difficult to (P)rovide for a need and (I)ntegrate simultaneously. I know this from my own experience. I have attended seminars where they talked about teamwork, interdependence, humanism and honesty. I always resolved to practice these concepts. But guess what? When I returned to work and suffered about twenty minutes of time pressure and conflict, I decided I had had enough (I)ntegration. Trying to be (I)ntegrative and at the same time task–

oriented is extremely difficult. My (I) role declines when my (P) role increases.

Any combination of the four roles is incompatible, not just *(P)* and *(I)*. (P)roducing and (E)ntrepreneuring are incompatible too. How many times have you said, "I'm working so hard, I have no time to think"? What does that mean? Pushing the rock, or satisfying present demands, is so overwhelming that you have no time to think about future opportunities. *(P)* actually endangers *(E)*.

Yes, I know. I've heard the saying, "People who work too hard have no time to make serious money."

Conversely, *(E)* threatens *(P)* too. (E)ntrepreneuring means change, and that threatens the *(P)* role. People in production often complain about research and development engineers or designers, saying, "If you guys don't stop changing things, we'll never get anything done." At some point, you have to freeze the planning so you can proceed with the doing.

This happens in some countries with a high rate of inflation. Democratic governments rise and fall frequently because of their economic problems. So governments change fiscal and monetary policies in an attempt to control inflation. But that might not solve the problems of inflation. In fact, it could make inflation worse. That's because people hedge their commitments when governments begin erratically changing their policies. They wait to see how, and if, things will stabilize. And the less people are committed to a plan of action, the less productivity, savings, and supply there will be. People might even transfer their financial resources to countries with more stability. Inflationary pressures will continue to rise. This in turn encourages more flights of capital and shaky commitments. To control inflation, stability is necessary.

Now let's look at another combination: *(P)* and *(A)*. They are also incompatible. Remember the tennis analogy we used in our previous conversation? When you want to be very effective, you have difficulty being efficient. And sometimes, if you are very efficient, you end up less effective.

(A) and (E) are also incompatible, right?

Sure. As you freeze new ideas for the sake of efficiency, your ability to proact and be effective in the long run will be inhibited.

We know that policies, rules, and institutionalized behavior inhibit change. Thus *(A)* endangers *(E)*. And vice versa; too much change hinders systematization, routinization, and order.

Another combination is *(P)* and *(I)*. We have talked about this incompatibility already. While trying to (P)roduce and (P)erform, that is, satisfy client needs, we might have to compromise the needs of some stakeholders. That can hurt (I)ntegration.

How about the (A)/(I) incompatibility, (A)dministration and (I)ntegration?

Let's explore this one with an example. Which country has the fewest lawyers per capita?

Japan, I think.

Correct. That means their need for (A)dministration is low and that is because their (I)ntegration is high. In Japan there is a great deal of loyalty and interdependence in business. Corporations offer lifetime employment and a family environment. They take care of each other; they are guided by their culture, not by their legal institutions.

Now which country has the most lawyers per capita?

The United States.

Yes! It seems as if everyone is suing someone. *(A)* is very high and growing; our court system is overloaded. We rely on external intervention to solve our interdependency problems. Our *(I)* is very low.

How did you conclude that (I) is low?

When you are highly (I)ntegrated, you feel as though you are fully joined with something or someone else. When does that happen? It happens when you love someone, and I'm not talking about sex or passion. I'm talking about the love of a parent for a child. If the child hurts, the parent feels as much if not more pain. The parent feels for the child as if they were one. Now think about this. Where do you see craving for love?

Probably in societies that are not (I)ntegrated.

Yes! As an example, look at the bumper stickers in California. Most of them are about love: "I love my dog," "I love my horse," I love, love, love. This preoccupation with love makes me suspicious that people don't have enough love in their lives. To find lonely people craving for love and a sense of belonging, go to big cities like Los Angeles.

And (I)ntegration or dis(I)ntegration occurs not only between people, or *inter*–people. We should look at (I)ntegration as *intra*–people, too.

Intra–people?

Yes. I use that word to describe (I)ntegration within a person, because there is more than one "me." There are several: mind, body, emotions and spirit. Frequently they are in conflict. The mind makes decisions that damage the body or the emotions. People often push their bodies to extremes while building a career. They work so hard their emotions also suffer. In modern society the mind receives most of the attention. The mind goes to school and earns a degree. If you measure what percentage of the day is allocated to the mind, you will find it gets the majority of our waking hours. Luckily, we sleep, so our body, emotions, and perhaps spirit enjoy some attention. But often the mind robs them of their share with sleepless nights.

Even if the body enjoys exercise, rest, and good food, the mind goes to school and earns a degree, and the emotions enjoy heart–to–heart communications, the spiritual part could still be deprived. The spiritual is best expressed when the body, mind, and emotions are quiet. If you fast for a while the body becomes quiet. If you meditate, the mind and emotions become quiet. Then you will get a deep sense of who you are. Your spirit will express itself. You will have a sense of unity within yourself and with the world around you. This could be a spiritual experience.

You may doubt this. *(I)* is difficult to explain because understanding one's spiritual nature is 100 percent experiential. For now, why don't you enjoy some poetry, music, or art? Or just watch nature. Experience something that doesn't speak to your mind, something that you don't try to understand. Experience something that makes you feel part of it. Experience love without trying to understand it. Love is not a cerebral, physical, or emotional experience. In its true form it is a spiritual experience, expressed in intimacy with something, someone or oneself.

What does this have to do with (PAEI)?

Well, the mind, body, emotions and spirit correspond to *(PAEI)*. Can you guess which role is represented by mind?

(A).

Body?

(P).

Emotions?

(E).

And spirit is *(I)*. Since these four roles are frequently in conflict, one of the roles might emerge dominant in our behavior. We might focus mostly on our body, mind, emotions, or spirit—whichever wins the internal battle at the expense of the others.

Change fuels our internal conflict. The more hustle and bustle in our lives, the less the four roles are in balance. The higher the rate of change we experience, the more the mind, body, emotions and spirit get scattered. Depending on a person's preference, usually expressed as a habit, one of the four roles wins, while the other three are neglected. Some people make their minds the master. These are the technocrats, the robot–like people with no emotions or spirituality. There are others who dedicate their lives exclusively to their bodies. Exercise and healthy food are their religion.

> *And the third group goes from one humanistic growth experience to the next, feeding mostly their emotional side. What about the exclusively spiritual group?*

They flock to the religious cults. The higher the rate of change in society, the more we see of such groups.

Where does this lead us?

The higher the rate of change, the more inter and intra–dis(I)ntegration, and that is expressed in lack of inter and intra–love.

Lack of inter–love. What is that?

Aggression, hostility toward others.

And lack of intra–love is aggression and hostility toward oneself?

Yes. The higher the rate of change, the higher the rate of depression and suicide.

So should we stop change?

No one has ever succeeded in doing that. People have slowed down change only to have it erupt with a vengeance later. Don't try to stop change. Learn how to deal with it instead.

How?

That's what our conversations are about. To start, note that (I)ntegration in its highest form is love, and loving others starts with loving yourself. That does not mean loving your mind *or* body *or* emotions *or* spirit, but loving your mind *and* body *and* emotions *and* spirit. Next, it means caring for the needs of others as if they were your own. That's why the group of friends can agree to go hiking together. That's why the leader is aware, conscious that the group would like to stop drinking and go hiking instead. Through the sense of (I)ntegration, this person can sense the emerging needs of the interrelating group. Since the different stakeholders have different needs, knowing how to (I)ntegrate them requires MODERATION, BALANCE, HARMONY, and SYNCHRONICITY of the components that make up the organization. And for that, conscious self–discipline is needed.

This conversation is a long way from comparing Japan and America. Where is your self–discipline?

You're right. Let's get back to specific differences between the *(A)* and the *(I)* roles, and why people should not substitute one for the other. Where were we?

We said Japan's advantage is strong (I), while the United States'
disadvantage is an increasing (A). We were discussing the (A) and
(I) incompatibility.

Okay. Where do you find more crime? In large cities with no community
spirit or in small places where people know each other?

In metropolitan areas.

If large cities where people are alienated suffer more crime, is it due to a
lack of *(P)*, *(A)*, *(E)*, or *(I)*?

(I), I presume.

And what is usually the attempted remedy? More...

(A).

Right! More law and order. More punishment. More prison time. Isn't it
bizarre they give people three or four life sentences when a person has
only one life to give? They electrocute or hang or inject lethal chemicals
into the sentenced criminal. Does this approach work to reduce crime?

No, it doesn't.

Because crime is not an *(A)* problem. It is an *(I)* problem. It is not a legal
problem. Inter and intra–dis(I)ntegration are causing it, whether it is the
individual who is dis(I)ntegrating and/or the surrounding political systems.

Wait! I am interested in business. We are spending too much time
on psychology, sociology, art, and religion. Can we get back to
business, please?

But we are discussing facets of life important to business. Think about
business students who only study how to use their minds. Little attention
is given to the needs of the body, or to controlling and enriching emotions
or spirit. Then, after they graduate and make a lot of money, they feel
lonely and deprived. They may accumulate art in an attempt to replenish

their spirit. Or maybe they go into therapy to treat their imbalanced emotions.

Isn't it better to live a balanced life, balanced up front and throughout, instead of continuously robbing *(I)* to pay *(P)*? When people are young they spend their health to make money. When they grow old, they spend their money attempting to regain their physical, emotional, and/or spiritual health. The same seems true for societies. In attempting economic growth, they destroy the environment, and frequently their spiritual and cultural heritage.

I agree, but you are out of balance. We said we were going to talk about mismanagement and what happens when (P), (A), (E) or (I) is missing. We've talked about everything but that.

You're right. Let me apply what I said about *(A)/(I)* incompatibility. The more (I)ntegration in a system, the less (A)dministration is needed. The more *(A)* type of court and legal intervention in our family and personal life, the less (I)ntegration and self–regulation is needed. Family dis(I)ntegration calls for government intervention, but that *(A)* intervention is causing family dis(I)ntegration too!

Are you saying, then, that the Japanese will lose their advantage if they bring more (A)dministration into their culture? Will an increase in (A) undermine their competitive advantage in (I)?

Yes.

Exporting (A) could be a way for the Americans to undermine the Japanese advantage. Teach them traditional American management theory: span of control, unity of command, management versus workers' rights. These practices would undermine their (I) advantage, right?

The United States doesn't have to export *(A)*. It can grow indigenously in Japan. As change accelerates, dis(I)ntegration could occur and they might attempt to control it with (A)dministration. They are not immune to such development because they have not articulated and systematized their cultural advantage *(I)* to the point that they can nourish and reproduce it. They are enjoying it while it lasts.

Why would they use (A) to control dis(I)ntegration and not (I)?

Because to (A)dminister a problem is so much easier than to (I)ntegrate a relationship. With *(A)*, you make a set of rules and your task is finished. Expression of *(I)* involves education and nourishment of culture and values.

> *That's right. It is easier to punish children than to teach them values of cooperation. I can see that. How about some more examples of (PAEI) incompatibility in business?*

Okay. Can you give me the *(PAEI)* code for the marketing function?

> *Well, first it should have an (E). Marketing has to analyze the future, how the clients and their needs will change.*
> *But before you identify the clients' needs you have to identify the clients and be conscious of their needs. That's (I).*

Congratulations. You are starting to master the *(PAEI)* code. And you've just hit on something critical. Without consciousness of needs, without a spiritual sense of interdependence, of oneness, without caring for the clients needs as if they were our own, we satisfy pseudo–needs. We might satisfy the client with pseudo–needs, and in the process we could make money, but we would also sabotage the total system. In the end, our efforts would come back to sabotage us.

Drug pushers are extreme manifestations of this phenomenon. How many people push what they know is damaging and continue to do so nevertheless? The proof that they know it is damaging is that they would not sell it to their own children they love. The owner of a factory that pollutes the air does not live or let the family he or she loves live where the factory is. But while drug pushers push things on our children, what is it that we push on their children? We must not do to others what we don't want others to do to us or to those we love.

> *"Love thy neighbor as thyself." Right?*

Yes, and, "Don't do unto others what you don't want done unto to you." Thus, true marketing, to be effective in the long run, has to be *(I)*–based. It must be *(I)* and *(E)*.

What else?

Third, it should have a *(P)*, because marketing has to (P)roduce results, not just analyze changes.

Okay. Anything else?

Last is *(A)*. The *how* is really the least important.

Now give me the (PAEI) code for the sales function.

How about if you do it.

First, it should be (P). Second, (E).

Why do you have *(E)* second?

Don't we want a creative, forward–thinking salesperson?

Yes, but that's not what we're talking about. We are not talking about a trader, contractor, or developer. We are talking about the sales *function*. On a personal level, a salesperson's personal style should be *(PaeI)*. And since *(P)* and *(I)* are very incompatible, outstanding salespeople are rare.

The question is the *(PAEI)* code of the sales *function* or sales *department*. *(P)* is most important because, in order to produce sales, a salesperson has to demonstrate how the product or service satisfies needs. But what should the second role be? Should the sales function be flexible, sensitive, or efficient?

Efficient. That's why we have sales territories, scheduling, itineraries, and routes—we want maximum bang for the buck.

Right! That's why it should be *(PAei)*, like a production function.

Come to think of it, it is like production. Marketing designs the plan—what should be sold at what price, and how it should be sold. Sales actually goes out and implements the plan. Stylistically, marketing is like process engineering and sales is like production.

And this *(PAEI)* code shows you the incompatibility between the styles and functions of marketing and sales. Marketing should be *(PaEi)*, while sales should be *(PAei)*. Marketing should look at the long run and make requests regarding what should be done to prepare for the future. Sales should be short–term–oriented and efficient. Marketing is change oriented and can disturb the order sales needs for short–term efficiency. So it's normal to have conflict between the sales and marketing departments of an organization.

> *You mean an excellent marketing person does not necessarily make an excellent sales person, and vice versa?*

Right.

> *Boy, then we sure make mistakes. In my company we usually promote the best salespeople into marketing.*

And to avoid conflicts, many companies put marketing and sales under the same manager. In government, the same mistake has been a major factor causing its bureaucratization. In my book *Corporate Lifecycles*, I discuss it further.[6] When marketing is put under the same vice president who is also in charge of sales, marketing has difficulty performing its function of providing leadership for change. It ends up performing mostly a support function, such as preparing sales collateral material. When production and engineering are combined, engineering usually performs a maintenance function.

> *Any other examples?*

How about the *(PAEI)* code for motivating?

> *(– – – I)?*

Why just *(– – – I)?* That couldn't be the code for motivating. You don't care what we do, or how or why we do it, just as long as we agree? That's not motivating. That's surrendering.

> *Is it (P) and (I)?*

No. What about the *(A)* and *(E)* roles? It's important that you not forget any role. Any deficiency will haunt you, because all four "vitamins" are necessary. Whenever one role is missing, one of the desired outcomes won't happen. The organization is going to be either ineffective or inefficient in the short or long run. Sooner or later, you will have to address the absent role if you wish to produce a healthy organization.

The Little League coach who inspires the kids with rah–rah–rah motivation saying, "Let's win this game!" is using a *(P – – I)* approach. Without *(A)*, there would be no systematized plan of how to win the game. Without *(E)*, there would be no plan of how to deal with future games. It would be only, "Let's unite, play hard, and win." Obviously, that could be enough for winning a game, but not the season.

Okay. All four roles are necessary. What about (pAeI)?

What kind of motivation do you think that would be?

It would be a system that motivates people, like a bonus or incentive program.

Right! And how about *(paEI)*? What kind of motivation is that?

When people have a vision of the future or a mission that motivates and unites them.

What type of motivation do we use most in the Western world?

I believe (pAeI).

Right again. Modern society is becoming increasingly *(A)* oriented. Jacques Ellul elaborates on this in his book *The Technological Society.*[7] Think about it. There is a manual on everything—on how to listen, talk, dress, eat, or make love. There is hardly a field of human endeavor for which there is no how–to manual. Even these conversations of ours can be converted into a manual on how to manage, lead, parent, or govern. But the strongest motivation is not *(pAeI)*; it is *(paEI)*. That's what people go to war for and die for. That's one of the reasons why Japanese productivity is so strong. People are hired there for the long run, so they identify with the long run vision. They know they will benefit from achieving the goals. They are motivated and thus dedicated.

> *This code is helpful. It is like shorthand. So what I've really learned today is that although all four roles are necessary, they are incompatible, and because of that, what?*

A role could be missing, squeezed out, threatened into extinction, or never fully developed. Next time, we'll discuss what type of mismanagement results when one or more of these roles is not performed.

> *That's nice, but you have not told me yet how to predict the quality of decisions?*

I promise we will get to it, and when we do, you'll see the trip was worth it. Happiness is not a destination. It is a journey. The same with learning.

Conversation 5

Mismanagement Styles

You know, I wish I had recorded our conversations. I feel I should listen to them many times to fully absorb them.

Yes, you should. To understand the totality of a system, you must view it from many angles. The beginning has more meaning after you know the end.

Okay. Let's see where we were. To manage is to decide and implement. To decide, we need to focus on effectiveness and efficiency in the short and the long run. For that we need the (PAEI) roles to be performed. The problem is that the roles are incompatible.
What happens if a role is not performed?

To understand what happens when a role is missing, I created archetypes of some extreme cases. In these cases, instead of having one role missing and three performed, I have three roles missing and one performed. Once we understand these extreme cases, we can better understand the less extreme ones.

The *(P – – –)*: The Lone Ranger

Let's take the first case, in which (P)erforming is the predominant role: it is the doing, the achieving, the single–minded fulfillment of the purpose for which the organization exists. *(A)*, *(E)*, and *(I)* do not exist in this *(P – – –)* style, which I will call the "Lone Ranger" style.

How does the Lone Ranger manage or lead? I emphasize the word *how*. We're not interested in *why* the *(P – – –)'s* style is as it is. We are not psychologists who want to know what happened in someone's childhood to cause certain behavior in adult life. We are interested in how someone actually behaves as a manager and what we can do about it.

Also, think about how the Lone Ranger rose through the ranks to become a manager.

> *That's easy. Diligent, hard working (P)erformers are often promoted to management.*

But now that several people are reporting to the Lone Ranger, what's happening?

> *There will be problems. (A)dministering, coordinating, and supervising are not a (P – – –)'s strong points.*

Neither are new ideas, change, and vision. (I)ntegrating people is also missing from the *(P – – –)'s* repertoire. This *(P)* excels exclusively in (P)erforming, in (P)roducing results.

> *I think I know this person.*

Let's examine the Lone Ranger's style. Does he or she work hard?

> *Certainly! Very hard.*

When does the Lone Ranger arrive at work?

> *First.*

When does he or she leave?

> *Last.*

There's a joke about this behavior. In inventory control, the terms LIFO and FIFO stand for Last In, First Out and First In, First Out. The Lone Ranger is neither a LIFO nor a FIFO, but a FISH...First In, Still Here. This (P) works all the time. At eleven o'clock at night, what does the (P – – –) take home?

> *A briefcase full of work.*

Right. The exhausted Lone Ranger might not have the time or energy to even open the briefcase, yet it's there next to the bed. Why?

> *Just in case...*

Some Lone Rangers travel the world lugging their briefcases. They don't have time to open them, but they carry them just in case. They're like alcoholics who are never far from a bottle. That's why some people call (P – – –)s workaholics, since they're never far from work. You can identify them in seminars. First of all, do (P – – –)s willingly attend workshops or seminars?

> *No. They go only if ordered to.*

Why?

> *Because they have no time. They have too much to do.*

At seminars, where do you find them during the break?

> *On the telephone to the office.*

And what are they saying?

> *"Any problems?"*

It's as if they're saying, "I've been here for two hours with, God forbid, no problems. Please give me a problem to solve." They're like alcoholics saying, "Two hours and I haven't had a drink. Please, have mercy. Give me a drink."

I know this type. When they are forced to attend a meeting and a secretary walks in with a stack of papers, they're the first to ask, "Anything for me?" They like to do. (P – – –)s measure themselves by how hard they work. They worry if they're not worried.

That's why it's dangerous to have a *(P – – –)* around after an organization has outgrown him or her. This person is like an unguided missile. Let's say the founder, the old papa, has a *(P) style* and he shows up at the office because he doesn't know how to fill his time any other way. If he has nothing to do, he will find something that may only stir up trouble. He might cross organizational boundaries and ignore organizational charts. You might even find him at the shipping dock telling people how to load a truck. Worse, he might call a customer and make a deal that violates company policies. Why? Because he has to do something. If you don't give this person something to do, he's going to do something you may not want done.

Lone Rangers work very hard. They complain that the day is too short and that there is too much to do. If someone asks, "Why don't you delegate some work to your staff?" what's the answer?

"They can't do it. They're not ready yet".

"How long have they worked for you?"

"Twenty-five years."

"So why don't you train them?"

"I have no time to train them!"

"And why don't you have time?"

"Because I have no one to delegate to."

They go in circles and can't delegate. That's why I call this person the Lone Ranger.

Next question: How does the Lone Ranger's desk look? Clean?

No, it's crowded with papers. If one desk is not big enough, there's a credenza behind it, also crowded.

And if that's not enough, there are papers all over the floor and along the wall. If you ask the *(P – – –),* "How are you doing?" what will the answer be?

"Oh my God! There's so much to do. I've been working so hard lately."

And if you ask how long "lately" is?

"Twenty-five years!"

Their behavior is compulsive. Imagine asking an alcoholic, "What should I do with this bottle of Chivas Regal?" What would he or she say?

"Put it on my desk."

Likewise, when you ask a Lone Ranger, "Boss, what should I do with this problem," what will be the response?

"Put it on my desk."

When you look at the desk of a Lone Ranger, what you see is not work but bottles. It's his or her wine cellar. If you want to see a scared Lone Ranger, clean up his or her desk overnight.

Interesting. I met a manager who had a subordinate who worked extremely hard but always complained she had too much to do. The manager decided to help her out by not giving her any new assignments until her desk was cleared. The cleaner the desk got, however, the more depressed she became. Instead of feeling relieved, she felt terrible. Now I understand why.

Good example. Now let's look at the people who work for a Lone Ranger. They come to work late and leave early. What are they doing in the meantime?

Waiting.

For what?

For an errand to run.

In organizational parlance, the Lone Ranger's employees are called "go–fers"; they go for this, go for that. They're untrained, unprepared, and undirected. They are expected to get it done and then ask, "What's next?"
Does the Lone Ranger hold staff meetings?

No.

Why not?

Because there isn't any time.

Suppose the Lone Ranger is told he or she must have staff meetings be-cause a good manager should have them. What would the meetings be like?

> *Very short. The Lone Ranger would tell the staff what to do, then send them on errands. Few questions would be asked. No debate. No discussion. Then the (P – – –) would proudly announce, "We had a staff meeting!"*

Next: Does the (P – – –), the Lone Ranger, train people?

> *No. A Lone Ranger would say, "I have no time to train," or "What is there to train people for? All they have to do is work hard and get the job done."*

The Lone Ranger sees the world in a simplistic way: "The problems are simple, the solutions are simple. The problem is you're not working hard enough. The solution is to work harder. That's all."

> *The (P – – –) confuses quantity with quality. More is better for a Lone Ranger. All you have to do is do more. "If we tried harder, we*

wouldn't have any problems. Our problem is that people are not working hard enough."

Function is everything; form is ignored. From the *(P – – –)'s* perspective if you work hard enough, success is assured.

The *(–A– –)*: The Bureaucrat

Let's proceed to the next deficient style. According to the code, it would be (–A – –).

What do you think the *(–A – –)* style is like? What does a blank in the *(P)* position mean, for instance?

The (–A – –) is not a (P)roducer of results, not a (P)erformer. He or she doesn't focus on the needs that must be (P)rovided, but solely on (A)dministration, systematization, and routinization. The Lone Ranger looks exclusively at what is being done, never mind how And the (–A – –) is looking exclusively at how it's being done, never mind what.

This person is not an *(E)*, who would move in new directions, take new risks, and initiate change. Neither is this person an *(I)*, who tries to bring people together. I call this person, an *(–A – –)*, the Bureaucrat.

A Bureaucrat manages by the book and looks exclusively at how to make the organization efficient.

Yes, and the book, by the way, doesn't have to be written. It may be all in the *(–A – –)'s* memory. He or she runs the organization on precedents. A system exists and you are expected to follow it. Everything must be documented. The Bureaucrat suffers from a disease called "manualitis"; everything must be put into manuals.

When does a Bureaucrat come to work?

On time.

When does he or she leave?

On time.

When do the Bureaucrat's subordinates get to work?

They'd better be there on time.

When do they leave?

On time.

What are they doing in the meantime?

That's not important. What's important is that they get there on time and leave on time.

That's how a Bureaucrat sometimes runs a well–controlled disaster. The company's going broke, but on time. Everything is very efficient and by the book.

And what does the Bureaucrat do with free time?

Write the book!

Yes! The Bureaucrat is always looking to control the number of violations. The (– A – –)'s function is to make new rules, new standard operating procedures and new policies. That's why in bureaucracies the book of procedures and policies grows larger and larger from year to year. The more violations the (– A – –)s find, the more rules they have to make. More rules, however, mean more violations, which means more rules are needed. The book grows over time without bringing more control.

The classic Bureaucrat is the character of Captain Queeg in *The Caine Mutiny,* by Herman Wouk. In the middle of World War II, what worries Captain Queeg most?

Who stole the strawberries.

A company managed by a Bureaucrat may be going broke, but they will call a meeting about who "stole the strawberries," or who did not fill out the proper form. The Bureaucrat wants to do things right and cares less about whether they are the right things. He or she would rather be precisely wrong than approximately right.

I can see that the Bureaucrat also confuses form with function, except that in contrast to the Lone Ranger, the Bureaucrat believes that if the form is carried out, the function will follow. An (– A – –) perceives that all that is needed to achieve results is to go through the motions.

Look at Captain Queeg. A typhoon was about to sink his ship unless he ordered a change in course. But what did he say? "I'm not disobeying orders on account of some bad weather."

This reminds me of a story about Bureaucrats. I was on a plane flying over the Amazon River in Brazil, and an accountant was seated next to me. He asked, "Do you know how old this river is? It's one million years and seven months old." That figure sounded strange, so I asked, "How do you figure one million years and seven months?" He said, "Well, seven months ago somebody told me it was a million years old." Bureaucrats will give you a budget balanced to the last cent, but in the wrong direction. They can be precisely wrong.

Your story reminds me of another one. Two friends were riding in a hot–air balloon and got lost in the clouds. They began to descend, trying to figure out where they were. When they spotted someone on the ground, they shouted to him, "Where are we?" The person shouted back, "In a balloon." One friend said to the other, "That guy must be an *(A)*. His information was accurate, precise, and totally useless."

I know that joke. There's more. The (A) on the ground went home and told his wife, "I just met two (E)s." The wife asked, "How do you know they were (E)?" The (A) answered, "They were flying high in the clouds and had no idea if they were coming or going."

Does a Bureaucrat have staff meetings?

Of course—probably every Monday, Wednesday, and Friday, from nine in the morning until noon.

Does the *(– A – –)* have an agenda?

Absolutely.

Dealing with what?

With details, with the how, not with the what and why.

And subordinates learn that if they don't make waves, do everything by the book, and lie low long enough, they might become the president.

Sad, but true.

Let's proceed to the third type of mismanagement, the one who practices *(– – E –)*. I call this person the Arsonist. How does this manager or leader behave?

The *(– – E –)*: The Arsonist
The (– – E –) has zero (P). He or she doesn't pay attention to providing the immediately needed service. He or she is also zero on (A); the details of how something gets done are unimportant. Zero (I) means interpersonal relationships, team building, and organizational climate are not important either. This person is an exclusive (E). The Arsonist is looking primarily to the future and positioning the organization to deal with change. The Arsonist is always creating and willing to take risks.

The time people arrive at and leave work is one of the behavioral characteristics that identify managerial or leadership styles. The Lone Ranger is first in, last out. The Bureaucrat is in on time, out on time. When does the Arsonist come to work?

Who knows!

When does he or she leave work?

Who knows!

An Arsonist is usually very dangerous on Monday mornings or upon returning from a plane trip that lasted more than three hours. The *(– – E –)* has had time to dream up new policies, new strategies, new priorities, and a new direction. The *(– – E –)* is very excited as he or she unloads these ideas on the employees. When do the employees come to work? What will happen if the *(– – E –)* shows up at seven in the morning and the employees are not there?

> *The Arsonist wouldn't like that. He or she would feel they're not committed enough.*

When do they leave?

> *Right after the Arsonist leaves!*

Yes, they have to be at work before the *(– – E –)* and leave after he or she does. But since they don't know when the Arsonist will appear or disappear, they are practically on call twenty–four hours a day, 365 days a year. It is not unusual for the Arsonist to call a staff member in the middle of the night from Paris to discuss a sudden idea.

> *I've seen companies with a big (– – E –) in charge. The subordinates are vice presidents who make huge salaries, but they just sit in their offices until seven or eight at night just watching their fingernails grow. They have little to do, but they're afraid to go home because the Arsonist might call a meeting. They never know when that might happen, but everyone must be ready. Nobody knows what the agenda is either. But even if the Arsonist does have one, he or she is the first to violate it. The staff is supposed to be able to answer questions according to whatever agenda the Arsonist has in mind. People attend meetings with their entire office in a mental suitcase.*

Let's compare this style with that of the Lone Ranger. The Lone Ranger is also called a workaholic. He or she might also be called a fire fighter, since the Lone Ranger responds to problems after they occur. When a fire flares up, he or she extinguishes it, then waits for the next burst of flames. Another term for the Lone Ranger is "manager by crisis." In fact, the Lone Ranger is managed by crisis.

Now, if the *(P – – –)* is a Lone Ranger and a fire fighter, the *(– – E –)* is an Arsonist. If the Lone Ranger's style is management by crisis, the Arsonist's style is crisis by management. If the Lone Ranger gets ulcers, the Arsonist gives them. That's why when the Arsonist returns from a trip, people whisper, "Heeeere he comes." They know the Arsonist will call a meeting and start new fires. And the Arsonist enjoys seeing people run around frantically, working harder than usual, as if the organization were on fire. That's why when an Arsonist asks you how you're doing, you should answer, "I'm working so hard, I'm falling apart. I haven't seen my family for weeks." The Arsonist might say, "Good, good."

In a company managed by an Arsonist, who does all the talking in a meeting?

The Arsonist!

Here's another joke to make the point. Italians are known for their food and their music, but not for their military accomplishments. In the First World War, some Italian soldiers were in the trenches ready to attack. Out of the trenches emerged a commanding officer in a beautiful blue uniform with a red sash, gold epaulets, and many decorations. He pulled out his saber, raised it to the sky and shouted, "Avaaaantiiiiiii!" The soldiers in the trenches looked up, clapped their hands, and shouted, "Bravoooo!" But nobody left the trenches!

The same happens in the organization managed by an Arsonist. Upon returning from a trip, the Arsonist calls a staff meeting and starts waving a saber in the air. He or she exclaims, we have this opportunity, we have that opportunity. We are going to do this, we are going to do that.

The subordinates look at each other and mentally clap hands while thinking, "Bravoooo! Heeeere we go again." But nobody gets out of the trenches. Why?

> *Because next Monday the Arsonist is going to change direction again. An Arsonist never tells you to stop what you're doing, but continues giving you new things to do. When people get out of the trenches, they soon realize they're running in circles. So what happens? They learn to stay in the trenches, clap their hands, and await the next avalanche of "absolutely top priorities." They pray and hope the boss will forget it. Maybe he or she doesn't really mean it. What does the (- - E -) really mean anyway?*

Subordinates spend an enormous amount of time trying to understand where their Arsonist boss stands. They waste energy trying to interpret directions and hold off on acting because they don't know if the decisions are for real. This frustrates the Arsonist, who has dreamed up more and more fantastic new ideas designed to make changes. Staff people cheer, "Bravo! Yes, we should do that." Yet they don't move. Nothing, or very little, gets done. The Arsonist grows impatient, thinking it's difficult to soar like an eagle when you're surrounded by turkeys. The organization is not moving, *(– – E –)* concludes, because the employees don't support what the Arsonist wants. Paranoia and suspicion of sabotage set in. The Arsonist fails to realize that people *can't* follow because they don't understand what is wanted. Arsonists, themselves, frequently don't know what they want either. They might even say, "It's too late for you to disagree with me. I've already changed my mind."

> *Sometimes subordinates think a decision is real, so they act on it. Then the Arsonist gets upset, asking, "Why did you do that? I was only thinking out loud." When they don't follow his or her directions, the Arsonist becomes outraged. "Why didn't you carry out my decision? That was a final, final decision!"*

People really have difficulty knowing what's going on with an Arsonist. They lose whether they work on an assignment or not. Without an easy way to carry out, or even catch up, with the latest idea, they constantly feel like losers. The Arsonist too suffers from a sense of failure. His or her mind rushes forward faster than the accomplishments of the organization, leaving them unfulfilled. Over time they feel disturbed and disillusioned, and deeply disappointed. Arsonists don't realize that they're their own worst enemies.

An organization is like a series of gears: a big wheel causes a succession of smaller wheels to turn. When the big wheel makes one turn, how many turns do the small wheels make?

Many turns.

If the "big wheel" is an Arsonist, it changes direction frequently and abruptly. It goes forward a full circle, then backward a half circle, then forward again a half circle, then back two full circles. What happens then to the small wheels? For every little bit the big wheel turns, they have to make a full circle. They turn a little, then in mid–turn they have to reverse. Before they even have a chance to follow the last instruction, they have to turn forward again. Finally, the gears break down. When they do, the Arsonist feels this proves his or her suspicion that the staff is not to be trusted. They did not do what they were supposed to do.

> *But Arsonists are charismatic. They're dreamers, and they attract people who believe in their dreams.*

Only to become disillusioned later, because people cannot fulfill their ever–changing dreams.

> *But wait, aren't we painting an extreme picture?*

Each one of these styles is an extreme case. *(P – – –)* is the Lone Ranger. When you have a big *(P)*, small (aei) it means the person is primarily a (P)roducer of results, but also has some ability in the other roles. He or she doesn't excel in them but isn't blind to them either. A *(Paei)* is not a Lone Ranger, but a (P)roducer, and usually a first line supervisor. By the same reasoning, a *(pAei)* is not a Bureaucrat but an (A)dministrator. And a *(paEi)* is not an Arsonist but an (E)ntrepreneur.

In life there are many combinations in roles. Different combinations of *(PAEI)* roles with different degrees of strengths and weaknesses produce styles that combine the archetypes described here.

Each style has strengths and weaknesses. We should not say that *(E)* is bad in itself. It's bad if the other roles are zero. We always have to ask ourselves if there is a full code. Does a particular person have a one–track style or a well–rounded style? We'll deal with this subject in more detail later on.

> *Okay, let's continue.*

Each of the extreme styles has a typical subordinate. As I mentioned, the Lone Ranger's subordinates are called go–fers. They're untrained and always ready to run errands. The Bureaucrat's subordinates are called yes–yes clerks. They follow the book and don't make waves.

The Arsonist's subordinates are called claques, like the people hired by an opera house manager to start artificial applause on opening night. An Arsonist's subordinates are paid to clap hands and cheer. When an Arsonist calls a meeting and presents ideas, can you object?

It's dangerous, because Arsonists will take it personally and hold it against you. Arsonists hire employees to clap hands, not to boo while they sing their high C. Tread lightly when disagreeing with Arsonists, because the big (E) also stands for Big Ego.

The moment you express doubts about an *(– – E –)'s* idea, he or she will interpret your reaction as disagreement. It would be better to preface your comments with, "I agree with you that...," and watch how you use the word "but." The Arsonist may get annoyed.

Now let's look at the last style of mismanagement, in which only the *(I)* role is performed. What happens when you have *(– – – I)*?

The *(– – – I)*: The Super Follower

This type of manager's exclusive focus is on "for whom", never mind what, how or why. They look at people and how they're dealing with each other.

Let me give you an example. Four people are looking out the same window, but they see four different things. One of them sees birds, mountains, lakes, and sailboats. Who is that? Who sees only the big picture?

The (– – E –).

The second person looks out the same window and sees no birds, no clouds, no sailboats—only that the frame is dirty. Who is that?

The (– A – –), the Bureaucrat.

Right. This style is obsessed with details. You could write a major report about how and why the company should enter the New York market, for instance, and the Bureaucrat might return it with small corrections and objections over minute details. You suspect the Bureaucrat missed the whole point of your report. You saw the big picture, and the *(– A – –)* missed it by focusing on the details.

The third person sees neither the big picture nor the details. Instead, this person is busy figuring out how the window opens and how it is cleaned. Does it allow enough air in? Is it facing the right direction? The functionality of the window is what interests this person most.

That's the (P – – –).

Right. And the last person isn't even looking at the window. This person is looking at the others and what they are looking at. Examining people and their interdependence is the primary concern of the *(– – – I)*. He is interested exclusively in "who is with whom". I call this person The Super Follower.

Why "Super Follower"?

Look at it this way. In a meeting managed by a Super Follower, who speaks?

Everybody else.

What does the Super Follower do?

Listens to which people said what, who did not say what, and why they didn't say what they could have said. He or she focuses on people and their interrelationships.

(I)s know what's going on politically better than everyone else in the organization. They have a good political nose. They don't show their cards easily because they want to know where the group is going before committing themselves. They don't communicate clearly because they want to find out first what other people think. They might send up a trial balloon by saying, "I have an idea, but I'm not that sure about it." They might say, "I recommend we declare dividends, but I don't feel too strongly about it." *(I)s* do not lead. They follow the followers.

There is another name for this style. When they translated my book *How to Solve the Mismanagement Crisis* into Spanish, they called this style *pez enjabonado*. That's Spanish for "Soaped Fish", something so slippery you can't hold onto it. In trying to corner the Soaped Fish, you might say, "You said this," to which he or she would respond, "You didn't understand what I really wanted to say." Soaped Fish always wiggle out. How? Because they are more politically astute than anyone else. They feel the vibrations and underlying currents of the organization before anyone else. Group dynamics and power politics are their focus.

Employees of the Soaped Fish are called informers. They find out what's going on, who said what, why they said what they said, and what they meant when they said it. Through these informers, the *(– – – I)* hears and understands the organizational drum signals.

We can sum up this conversation about managers and mismanagers with this chart:

(Paei) = (P)roducer	*(P– – –)* = **Lone Ranger**
(pAei) = (A)dministrator	*(–A – –)* = **Bureaucrat**
(paEi) = (E)ntrepreneur	*(– –E –)* = **Arsonist**
(pael) = (I)ntegrator	*(– – – I)* = **Super Follower**

This was an entertaining discussion. What's next?

Let's stop for today. We have learned that when any of the *(PAEI)* roles is missing, mismanagement will occur and the resulting style of mismanagement will be somewhat predictable. Next time, let's discuss what happens when all four *(PAEI)* roles are missing or when all four *(PAEI)* roles are performed equally well.

That should be easy.

It isn't, and you'll see why.

Conversation 6

What to Do About Change

Would you like to summarize our last discussion?

> *Sure. You said we need all the (PAEI) code performed in order to make good decisions.*
>> *Good decisions are necessary for solving problems.*
>> *Problems emerge because of change.*
>> *Change is constant.*
>
>> *If one or more of the (PAEI) roles are missing, a predictable mismanagement style will emerge. We have already discussed the four extreme styles, the (P – – –), (– A – –), (– – E –) and (– – – I). Now, what about a manager who has zero (P), zero (A), zero (E), and zero (I)? What type of style would four blanks indicate?*

(– – – –): Deadwood
I refer to a manager with none of those roles as Deadwood. Deadwood mismanagers are not interested in *what, how, why,* or *who,* but only in survival. Low managerial metabolism and low energy are their trademarks. They say "Uhm uhm" and "yes, yes" a lot, but never actually do much.

Deadwood never shows resistance to change either. Remember how the other mismanagers resist change? If Lone Rangers are told to change something, they'll say, "How can I do it? My desk is full," or " I'll get to it when I have time."

Why do Bureaucrats resist change? Because they know the cost of everything and the value of nothing. They dwell on the repercussions of change, so they say it can't be done. "It's too risky" or "It's too costly." They think from an implementation point of view and perceive opportunities as problems.

Arsonists resist change when the idea is not their own. And Super Followers oppose new ideas because those ideas could be politically risky. "People aren't ready for it yet. This is not the right time." The "right time" for them is not when the market demands it, but when the internal political climate will allow it.

Deadwood has a different attitude about change. If you tell a Deadwood manager, "Let's move Denver to the Sahara," he'll say, "Sure." No up–front resistance. But a year later when you ask, "Where are we with the project to move Denver to the Sahara?" he'll say, "We've been studying it. Here's a preliminary report. We're still working on it." You see! He didn't move one pebble to the Sahara. But the Deadwood spent plenty of his time just protecting himself for not moving one pebble anywhere.

It's very difficult to get rid of Deadwood, because they always agree with you and accept any assignment. They always say, "Everything's okay! Whatever you say! Sure!" But they don't do anything and feel perfectly all right about it. When someone gets fired, the Deadwood might say, "I don't know why they fired Lisa. She didn't do anything."

Another characteristic that distinguishes the various types of mismanagers are their typical complaints. For instance, Lone Rangers say...

"Too much work to do. I'm not catching up."

Bureaucrats...

"It's not being done the way it should be. It's not properly organized or under control." They emphasize the word "should."

How about Arsonists?

"People are not following the priorities. They're working on the wrong tasks." Arsonists complain even though they constantly change the priorities so many times that nobody knows knows what the latest priorities are.

What about Super Followers?

"We don't communicate well. You must have misunderstood me. What I really meant to say was..."

In contrast, the Deadwood doesn't complain. "How is it going?" "Fine."

Look again at the characteristics of the Deadwood disease: low managerial metabolism, no resistance to change and no complaints. But none of these traits are fatal. What makes Deadwood really dangerous is that the disease spreads. Deadwood multiplies.

What do you mean?

Every one of these mismanagers has a typical subordinate, and who do you think works for Deadwood?

More Deadwood.

Yes. My greatest fear when diagnosing an organization is when I ask how it's going, everyone answers "Everything is fine. No problems." Remember, the quietest place in town is the graveyard; nothing happens there; no one has any problems because there is no change. That's death. Being alive means change, and change means working on problems, and growing means working on larger problems.

But why does Deadwood multiply?

Deadwood doesn't grow in managerial capabilities. It doesn't move on or delegate. This keeps the people under Deadwood from growing as well. When Deadwood dies managerially, the people below will eventually die as well. Efficiency and effectiveness disappear and no one knows why, because no one is complaining. When managers tell you *everything* is okay, and when no one is trying to improve or change anything, the organization has too much Deadwood.

But why does Deadwood appear? What can we do about it?

If you look at the previous four styles—Lone Ranger, Bureaucrat, Arsonist, and Super Follower—you can see that the difference between those styles and the Deadwood is the number of blanks they have in their *(PAEI)* codes. Deadwood has four blanks. The others each have three. Thus the first four styles are three–quarters Deadwood already.

(P – – –)	=	**Lone Ranger**
(– A – –)	=	**Bureaucrat**
(– – E –)	=	**Arsonist**
(– – – I)	=	**Super Follower**
(– – – –)	=	**Deadwood**

Lone Rangers become Deadwood when they lose their exclusive capability, which is to (P)roduce results.

How does that happen?

Lone Rangers work very hard and claim they have no time to train subordinates. But who else do they not have time to train?

Themselves.

So what happens after twenty years? They are not people with twenty years of experience, but rather people with one year of experience repeated twenty times. They still work hard, but they are obsolete. The world has changed and they haven't adapted.

How do Bureaucrats become Deadwood?

They manage by the book. If you want to "kill" them managerially, change the book: computerize the company, install new budgetary systems. If the Bureaucrat can't adapt, a major change could transform him or her into Deadwood.

How about Arsonists?

They burn out when they start one fire too many and can't control them anymore. Soon they lose the trust and respect of the people who work for them. The organization eventually stops listening to the Arsonist, who still has ideas but no followers. Eventually Arsonists lose faith in themselves and stop trying.

And Super Followers?

They become Deadwood when a crisis demanding immediate resolution arises and they cannot solve it the *(I)* way, because (I)ntegration of people requires time and there is no time. What usually happens is that a small revolution erupts from below and they are pushed aside. The situation calls for action, not negotiation. They still might try to (I)ntegrate, but nobody will listen anymore.

Do you see the common denominator in all four cases?

Let me think. Lone Rangers becomes Deadwood when there is change and they don't adapt. Bureaucrats become Deadwood when the system of implementation changes and they can't handle it. Arsonists become Deadwood when they spur too much change and lose control. Super Followers become Deadwood when a crisis requires immediate action and they lose control of the political process.

The common denominator is change!

Exactly. Show me an organization with a high rate of change and I will show you a growing heap of Deadwood.

Hmm! But that's not a typical bureaucracy where change is slow and thus I would expect to find Deadwood. Are you referring to a bureaucracy experiencing fast change through deregulation?

Yes. In a regulated environment everything *appears* under control. The Deadwood beneath the surface bursts forth when regulation is removed and change is introduced rapidly.

Actually, the organization which is subject to the highest degree of Deadwood is a rather young company going through tremendous change, perhaps a high–tech company. Unless it invests heavily in retraining, it will have either a high turnover or growing Deadwood. It changes so fast that some people cannot keep up. They die managerially.

On the macro level the same phenomenon might occur. Show me a society with a high rate of change, and I will show you a society with many homeless people. Their plight is not due to unavailable employment. When a society changes rapidly, many people cannot keep up. They cannot work effectively and gainfully in such an environment. They simply give up.

Why are there so many homeless people in the United States, the richest country in the world? Because the USA is undergoing tremendous change. The same is true of developing nations. Countries that are industrializing rapidly have streets full of beggars.

But the USA is already industrialized.

The USA is moving into the post–industrial age. There is a change from manufacturing and service industries to knowledge–based industries. These fields require more brainpower than muscle, and some people cannot link up with those changes.

Do you suggest we stop change?

No one can stop change, although many individuals, political parties, and religious movements have tried. The way to handle change is not by slowing change down, but by learning how to solve the problems of change faster.

Any suggestions?

I found that change follows a predictable pattern, which means that problems have a predictable pattern too. Change follows a lifecycle, and certain problems are indigenous to each phase of the lifecycle. Some of these indigenous problems are normal and some are not. The role of management is to remove the problems inherent to the phase of the lifecycle the organization is in, and prepare the organization to deal with the problems that will come with the next stage. To learn more about organizational lifecycles, I again refer you to my book *Corporate Lifecycles*. What is clear for our discussion now is that decisions need to be made for solving the problems that emerge with change. Those decisions must provide solutions that will make the organization effective and efficient in the short and long run. This means we need a *(PAEI)* decision. To get a *(PAEI)* decision we need the *(PAEI)* roles to be performed, which means we need a *(PAEI)* style.

The styles we have been discussing constitute mismanagement because they are missing one or more of the *(PAEI)* roles. What do we need to make good decisions that will make organizations effective and efficient in the short and the long run?

We need a person with a complete (PAEI) style.

We need someone who is task–oriented and organized, systematic and thorough. He or she must have a global view and be creative and willing to take risks. Further, he or she must be sensitive to other people's needs, a person who is a team builder, who makes himself or herself dispensable.

But such a person doesn't exist.

Exactly! This *(PAEI)* manager exists only in textbooks. By the same reasoning, there is no perfect parent, perfect, manager, or leader, and for that matter a perfect flower. Nothing is ever perfect in itself when it is subject to change. Perfection occurs only when time is irrelevant. That's why we say that art is timeless (until we eat the fruit of that second tree of Eden). None of us is perfect. Now you can relax. You and I and all of us are imperfect. So what's new? People have been chasing this myth of the perfect manager for years by raising salaries, increasing stock options, and giving all kinds of special rewards to CEOs. All in a quest to find this incredible faultless genius. This utopian expectation gives rise to the errant direction of much management education in the United States. The existing programs describe what managers *should* do, although in reality they cannot do it. Open any textbook on management theory, and you will find that the most repeated word is *should*. The manager *should* plan, *should* organize, *should* communicate, *should* discipline, *should* lead. The fact is no one can excel in everything. Why? The managerial process is far too complicated for any single individual to perform alone.

Because the (PAEI) roles are incompatible, no one can be (P), (A), (E), and (I) at any one time, let alone forever.

If the *(PAEI)* manager exists only in textbooks, does that mean every organization will be mismanaged?

No.

Why not?

Because although no individual can be the perfect manager, we can have a team.

Right. But watch out. Not just any team. It must be...

A complementary team.

Right. What is necessary is not a single omnipotent genius, but a complementary team. I emphasize the word *complementary*. Often, when I use the word *team*, people say, "Right. I need a team of people like me." That's not team building. That's cloning.

Look at your hand again. A hand is five *different* fingers, which together act like a hand. If all the fingers were alike, you wouldn't have a hand. In management, we need a complementary team with a sense of *united differences*. If all the components were the same, the organization would be vulnerable. If they were different, the organization would still be vulnerable because the differences would work at cross purposes. Strength comes from *united differences:* different fingers with different distinct capabilities that work together.

The same holds true for a society. The society that is going to handle change best is one that has complementary cultures. I'm not talking about complementary abilities and knowledge, but complementary styles and judgments.

But don't these differences create miscommunication and conflict?

There are many reasons for miscommunication. This is one of them. When people's styles are different, they can miscommunicate easily.

So how can united differences give strength? Differences lead to conflict, and conflict is a weakness.

On the contrary, differences can give strength.

You'd better explain that one.

Differences are a strength if, when united, they compensate for each other's weaknesses.

I see. They have to be united. But how do you accomplish that?

Let's start from the beginning and find it together. First, no single person or any single culture or religion is perfect. Thus, what we need is a complementary team or a complementary society.

Right.

A complementary team or society, by definition, means differences in styles and cultures.

Right.

Differences mean potential conflict.

Right.

So conflict is necessary and inevitable in the management of change. Anytime we try to eliminate conflict, we're not managing well. We're like the would-be sailor who says, "I would like to cross the ocean and visit foreign lands, but I don't like big waves." So this "adventurer" stays at home, sits in the bathtub, and reads travel magazines.

It's the same phenomenon when managers or political leaders say, "I love to manage or lead. It's people I can't stand." They are sitting in their managerial bathtub, avoiding the real task of management or leadership: the harnessing of conflict.

The higher the rate of change is, the higher the rate of conflict. Socialist theorist Karl Marx lived during the Industrial Revolution, a time of rapid change. He witnessed the conflict it created, so he preached the negation of conflict through a classless society with a unity of interests—united workers, farmers and intelligentsia. The application of his theories stopped a lot of conflict, but what else did it stop?

Change.

Right. The Soviet Union began to fall behind technologically, socially, economically, even artistically. Mikhail Gorbachev had to enable change.[8] But the moment he did, what else had to occur?

Conflict.

Right. There is no change without conflict, and if you try to stop one, the other will stop too.

If you don't like managing conflict, don't try to be a manager or a leader. If you don't like people or handling differences of opinion, then get out of the manager's hot seat. Managing is, in large part, dealing with people who have different styles. People have different opinions that must be united. We can now add this element to our master diagram.

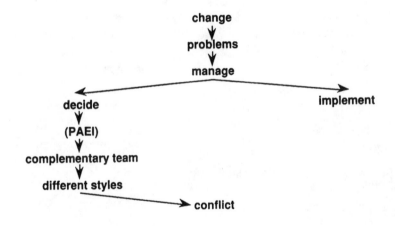

I understand conflict is necessary. But can't it be destructive instead of constructive? Not all conflict is desirable.

Let's think about when it would be constructive. Wouldn't you say that conflict is constructive when it is synergistic, when the whole that is developed through disagreements is better than the accumulated differences?

Yes.

And when would it be synergistic? When you learn from dissenting opinions, right?

Right.

And when do you learn from someone who disagrees with you?

Only when I respect what that person has to say.

Anytime you are grappling with a complicated subject—regarding your career, business or personal life—you consult someone for an opinion. However, you cannot learn from just anyone.

Why consult someone who is just like you, who always agrees with you? If you find someone who is different from you, but you don't respect that person, again you will not learn. When seeking advice you should look for someone who will complement you *and* someone you respect. Conflicts are synergistic when they are growthful. They are growthful only when learning occurs, and that happens only when there is mutual respect.

Let's go over this one more time. When you have a problem you cannot solve alone, you should consult someone whose decision–making style is different from yours. But would you go to just anyone who disagrees with you?

Obviously not. I would consult only someone whose opinion I respected.

Yes! And when would you respect a difference of opinion?

When I get something out of it.

When you *learn* from that difference of opinion. If you go to someone who has a different opinion, but find you haven't learned anything that changed your position, then you will feel you wasted your time. You don't respect what that person has to offer.

I've heard something like this before: "When two people agree on everything, one of them is dispensable." Also, there's a Zen saying, "If everyone in a meeting agrees on everything, none of them is thinking too hard." We enrich ourselves through differences, and we learn from differences, as long as we respect those differences. But isn't the handling of differences painful?

Granted. Working together in spite of differences is painful, but the pain produces gain. Once you see this, you will continue to seek people who are different from you not in spite of their differences, but because of them.

What kind of people are you talking about?

Colleagues. I define colleagues as people who disagree with you but whose opinion you respect. Such disagreement is called collegial disagreement, which is based on mutual respect. You respect their differing position because you learn from it.

The word *colleague* comes from the Latin words "arrive together." Colleagues may start from different points of view, but by interacting they arrive together at the same point of view. For colleagues it's not where you start from that counts but where you end up. It is not the conclusion that validates the process, because the conclusion is going to change over time. It is the process that legitimates the results. How we arrive at a conclusion in a climate of mutual respect is an asset that can be reapplied, while the conclusion or solution can change with time. As President Dwight D. Eisenhower once said, "Plans are useless. Planning is priceless." In Hebrew, the root consonants of the words *colleague* and *confrontation* are the same. Therefore, a colleague is someone with whom you are necessarily in disagreement. Colleagues teach each other by disagreeing respectfully.

Now I'd like to broaden the focus of the discussion by examining the importance of respect in modern society. I believe the world stands at a major intersection on the path of history. Because of change, the problems facing society as well as individuals are increasingly complex. The difference between the styles and cultures, which means differences in opinions on how to solve society's problems, causes conflict within a person as well as between societal groups and countries.

Whether a person or a society—our global society—will emerge stronger or weaker because of change depends on how we handle our differences. If we build a society of colleagues who respect and capitalize on each other's differences through democracy, we will emerge stronger, and there is no democracy without mutual respect. The decisions a democracy makes are not as important as the method used to make them. If a decision turns out to be a mistake, a democratic system that encourages criticism and debate can rectify it. The system enables change, and what it means to be a democratic society has to change democratically too. The higher the rate of change, the more democratic the system must be at every level.

What about applying this to the individual.

Individuals should have self-respect for the differences of opinion they have within themselves. They have to recognize and accept the fact that no personal decision is permanent. Keeping an open mind with oneself and with others is essential to making good decisions. Being one's own colleague is the essence of personal success.

Can we go back? I need to review this.

Okay. Since the textbook manager does not exist, we need a complementary team in which the team members respect each other's differences and make decisions based upon that respect.

Does the team have to have four people representing each of the four (PAEI) roles?

Not necessarily. You can have as few as two people. For example, one person who is *(PaEi)* and another who is *(pAeI)* can make an effective complementary team. By the way, this combination is often called a Mom and Pop store. Traditionally, who is the *(PaEi)* in a small family business? Who is the one who opens new stores, brings in new products, and decides on new prices?

The Papa.

Right. Traditionally the Mama keeps the books, an *(A)* function. She also performs the *(I)* function. She might warn a client, "Come tomorrow. He's a little bit crazy today." It's no coincidence they call it a Mom and Pop store. There are times, however, when the Mom and Pop roles overlap, or they even exchange roles. Remember, men are not "inherently" (P)erformers, and women are not inherently (A)dministrators and (I)ntegrators.

Why can't it be called just the Mom store or the Pop store?

Because there is no successful Pop without a complementary Mom, and vice versa. It takes a complementary team to build a store or to build a family. Show me a successful company, and I'll show you a complementary team. Show me a successful society and I'll show you different cultures working together in a climate of mutual respect.

I suggest that the United States is successful not just because of its vast physical resources—there are countries with just as many resources—but because it benefits from its socio–political culture of mutual respect and trust. It recognizes and respects cultural differences. Have you ever seen a street celebration of America's heritage? Every nationality that makes up the American population is represented, including nations with whom America was at war. Equal opportunity is the law. Oppressed people from around the world come to the United States for the opportunity to succeed. Discrimination on the basis of race, creed or sex is prohibited by law. If discrimination should increase in the United States, it's strength would diminish.

So how do we handle these differences?

We have to legitimize differences and unite them through a system of mutual respect. We are then enriched *because* of these differences, not in spite of them. Learning is nurtured because mutual respect encourages the cross–pollination of ideas.

When will differences be constructive and synergistic? When will they produce a learning environment? When there is mutual respect. Without it, there is no learning, and with no learning, conflict is dysfunctional. Without mutual respect, disagreements are pain with no gain.

Conflict is necessary because a complementary team is needed for making *(PAEI)* decisions. *(PAEI)* decisions are necessary for any system to be effective and efficient in the short and long run, whether it's an organization or a society. There is no textbook manager, just as there is no perfect political party, perfect religion, or perfect culture. A complementary team or society, by definition, comprises individuals or cultures who think and behave differently. That creates conflict, which is desirable when functional, and it is functional when it is based on mutual respect. Let's add mutual respect to our diagram.

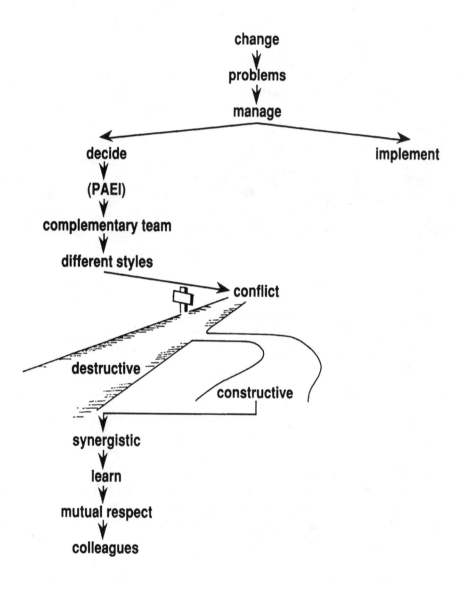

Good decisions, therefore, are a function of a complementary *(PAEI)* team and mutual respect.

$$\text{quality of decisions} = f \left\{ \begin{array}{l} 1.\ \text{(PAEI)} \\ 2.\ \text{mutual respect} \end{array} \right\}$$

Wait! I think I've got it. The two questions I should ask before opening the envelope from our earlier exercise are: Who worked on the problem and How did they work on it.

Right, and if you don't have a *(PAEI)* complementary team...

...or mutual respect, then don't open the envelope. You have the wrong problem and the wrong solution.

If the team were four (A)s, you could predict they would see the problem as a lack of systems of control, and their solution would be to institute more standard operating procedures.

If they were four (I)s, they probably decided to appoint a subcommittee to study the issue further. They would wait to see which way the wind was blowing.

If they were four (P)s, the meeting was very short. The solution would also be simple—fire, sell, or something like that.

If they were four (E)s, don't even go near the envelope.

Right. Their solution would probably create twelve more problems. Arsonists' solutions create side effects.

And if you have a complementary team of two or more in which all four roles were performed, what would the next question be?

How did the team work together?

Right. If they say they disagreed a lot but compromised to meet a deadline...

Don't open the envelope. There was no mutual respect.

But if they say they disagreed but learned from each other, so that by the end they came up with a solution they all supported...

Then open the envelope. Great. But there must be more to it. Do they vote or must they have a consensus?

We'll discuss that later. The important thing now is to note that what allows us to predict the quality of decisions is the styles of the people who make them and the quality of their interactions.

For good decisions we need a complementary *(PAEI)* team that works with mutual respect.

I think I understand this well now. Thank you. Let's proceed to the efficiency of implementation.

We'll do that the next time.

Conversation 7

Responsibility, Authority, Power and Influence

Have you done anything with what we discussed in our last few conversations?

I definitely have. Now I look at people and say that lady is a (P) or that guy is an (A).

Wait, wait, wait. That's not right. You're branding people like cattle.

What's wrong with that? Don't you have tests to measure (PAEI)?

No, I don't, although there are psychological tests to determine personality types. It can be done by anyone familiar with the work of Carl Jung. After I developed the *(PAEI)* model, people told me it paralleled some of Jung's theories. I was previously not aware of that. In any case, since my model is similar to Jung's, you can use the Meyers–Briggs test, among others, to measure *(PAEI)*.

So if these tests exist, what exactly is your objection to testing and, as you say, "branding" people?

I claim that people's behavior is conditioned mostly by environment. If you assign someone an *(A)* task, that person will behave like an *(A)* even if he or she is an *(E)* at heart. So what good is knowing what a person is at heart? I am interested in the impact someone's behavior has on others.

Don't you want to know someone's personality type for hiring purposes?

Absolutely. People who make staffing decisions should use tests, but staffing is not the concern here. I try to change people's behavior, and my approach is not by restaffing but by changing the environment in which they work.

For instance, don't say that someone *is* a *(P)*, rather say that person *behaves* like a *(P)*. Instead of administering a test, watch how a person behaves.

What's wrong with labeling people?

If you do that, your tendency will be to change the *people* rather than the *environment* that causes people's behavior. Before we go any further why don't you summarize our past conversations.

Sure. We need to manage because there are problems that need to be solved. There are problems because there is change. In order to solve problems, we have to decide what to do and we have to implement the decisions we made.

To make good decisions means to make decisions that make the organization effective and efficient in both the short and the long run. For that to happen we need all the (PAEI) roles to be performed. If any one of the (PAEI) roles is not performed, the organization will be mismanaged in the short or long run, or both, depending on which role is missing.

So we must be certain that all the (PAEI) roles are realized. The problem is that no one person can perform all the four (PAEI) roles together and over time, because they are incompatible.

Therefore, we need a complementary team. This necessarily means conflict because of the differing styles that compose such a team. This conflict is constructive when it is synergistic. For there to be synergy there must be learning. For learning to occur there must be mutual respect between the people. People who disagree respectfully and who learn from each other are called colleagues.

The quality of a decision can be predicted by looking at whether it was made by a complementary (PAEI) team and whether there was mutual respect between the members of the team.

Good summary!

You said we would discuss implementation today. How can we know if a decision will be implemented?

In order to predict whether or not a decision will be implemented, certain factors must be analyzed. First, you cannot implement a decision that's not well–defined. If the decision is ambiguous, it's not going to be implemented the way you want .

What do you mean by "well–defined"?

You cannot have an *almost* well–defined decision. It's either well–defined or it isn't. A well–defined decision is one that fulfills the four imperatives of decision making.

What are they?

They are the imperatives corresponding to the *(PAEI)* roles. Fulfilling them gives you a *(PAEI)* decision.

A (PAEI) decision?

Yes, the *(P)* role fulfills the first imperative: *what* to do. Can you guess what imperative the *(A)* role fulfills?

How to do it.

(E)?

Why.

Yes, but interpreted in the *when* imperative. The timing of a decision is derived from the reason for making that decision in the first place.

What about *(I)*?

Who does it.

Yes. And *why* drives them all when the *when* is its own derivation.

I see. Why drives what to do, how to do it, when to do it and who does it.

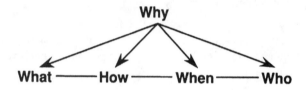

Right. When we make our decision, we need to decide (1) what to do, which is fulfilled by the *(P)* role; (2) how to do it, fulfilled by the *(A)* role; (3) when to do it, fulfilled by the *(E)* role; and (4) who should do it, fulfilled by the *(I)* role. We must satisfy the four *(PAEI)* roles if we want to have a well-defined decision.

Frequently people believe they've made a decision, but in reality they've decided only one of the four imperatives. Usually they decide *what* to do without deciding *how*. Later on, they may discover that *how* the decision was implemented has undermined *what* was decided. The *how* destroyed the *what*.

Give me an example.

You probably know this from experience with your kids. They ask if they can do something, and you say yes. Later, they did *what* you approved of, but *how* they did it makes you wish you had never approved the decision in the first place.

That's true. Sometimes my spouse doesn't tell me what to do, only how to do it. But by the time she finishes telling me in full detail how to do it, she de facto has told me what to do. The what and the how are interrelated. I can see that.

When is also important. If the decision is not carried out in time, the decision will no longer be valid. *Who* should do it is also important. Sometimes, the person to whom you assign a task determines how the decision will be implemented. Different people interpret decisions to fit their style.

You mean a decision is not well–defined until the what, how, when and who are communicated and understood? Only then is the decision clear. Right?

If you decide only one of the *(PAEI)* imperatives, the person who is assigned to implement the decision will have to provide his or her own interpretation of the other three imperatives. Then he or she will do it according to his or her own style. As a result, you might not like the way the decision was carried out.

So, if I want to predict whether a decision will be implemented correctly, I should check whether the four imperatives were clearly stated and understood. This sounds logical and reasonably simple. Why don't people follow this procedure when making all decisions?

Because people have different *(PAEI)* styles. Lone Rangers, or *(P – – –)s*, usually look at the *what* and don't invest time to articulate the *how*. *When* is usually *now!* and *who* is probably whoever is available right then and there.

Bureaucrats, or (A)dministrators, usually look at the *how*. They drive the *what* and *when* by *how* it should be done.

Arsonists, or (E)ntrepreneurs, are interested in the *why not* and the *when*. They give you the general idea and usually want it done yesterday. Ask them *what* we should do and watch them answer you with *why* they want it done.

(I)ntegrators, or Super Followers, are more interested in *who* is going to do it than in *why* it needs to be done. For them, the *what, how* and *when* are driven by *who*.

That's why a decision will usually have one imperative decided and finalized, while the other imperatives remain ambiguous or not expressed at all. The imperative adopted depends on which style dominates the decision making process. In order to have a good decision implemented, all four imperatives must be finalized and communicated. This requires a true complementary team that works with mutual respect.

So I must have a decision for which the (PAEI) imperatives are communicated and understood. Is that all there is to having a well–defined decision?

Not yet. It must be bound, too.

What does that mean?

Visualize a decision as a square. In each of the four corners is one of the *(PAEI)* imperatives that define a decision.

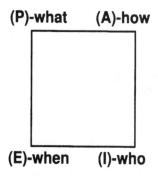

(P)-what   (A)-how

(E)-when   (I)-who

But a square is more than four corners. It has another physical characteristic: it binds space.

Inside the square is the *what* we can do, *how* we can do it, *when* we should do it, and *who* should do it. Outside the square is what *not* to do, how *not* to do it, who should *not* do it and when it should *not* be done.

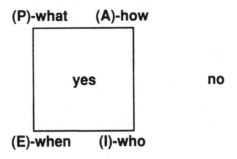

What are you saying?

I'm saying that you don't know what to do until you know what not to do. Consider this example given by Professor Herbert Simon, Nobel Laureate in economics. Jennifer is trying to teach Tom how to lace his shoes. A curtain separates them. Tom does exactly as Jennifer directs, but he misinterprets in every possible way. Jennifer says, "Take the shoelace and put it through the first hole, and then from below through the second hole." Tom does exactly that, except he passes the shoelace around his shoe first. Jennifer cannot tell Tom how to lace his shoe correctly unless she *realizes* what Tom is doing and can tell him also what *not* to do.

Anytime something new is attempted, people must learn what not to do as they attempt to do it correctly. A person really knows what to do only when he also knows what not to do, and that knowledge comes with experience.

It is the same with the *who* component. We learn from experience *who* should perform a task after we make the mistake of assigning it to someone we found to be the wrong person. We know better *who should* perform a task after we learn *who should not* do it.

Is that why, for some people, their second marriage is better than their first?

If they learned from their experience. Good experience comes from good decisions. Good decisions come from good judgment and good judgment comes from bad experience. What I'm saying is that you do not learn from what's *ex*pected, but what is *in*spected. Through inspection you get feedback. That's how you learn from mistakes.

I know which managers manage by expectations only: the Arson-ists. They make a decision and expect the task to be accomplished. They hate to inspect, follow through and make corrections. As their name suggests, they wind up starting fires and creating problems.

Right. Managers should analyze the results of their decisions. Inspect them and learn from experience. Analyze them until they know what to do and what not to do, how to do and how not to do, when to do and when not to do, and who should do it and who should not do it. Only then can they have a decision that is fully defined and understood.

But by that time, most probably, the decision is obsolete. They'll have to start all over again.

Right. Life is live and learn. Constantly! There is really no such thing as a good decision, it's only a good decision "for the time being." It takes time to experiment with a decision until it works. But even then, don't become too attached to it. Its life span is short. The higher the rate of change, the shorter the time span for the validity of the decision.

Got it. Please continue.

A decision has to be depicted graphically as a square. It has to be bound, and it must have four imperatives. The square represents the decision that is supposed to be implemented: the defined responsibility. A person can't be really responsible until he or she has a well–defined *(PAEI)* task, which means a square of responsibility.

But many times even if we know the four imperatives, the decision will still not get implemented. Why?

The *(PAEI)* imperatives are the first factors that predict implementation, but not the only ones. We also need "managerial energy" to carry the decision through. Often we know what needs to be done, but we can't carry it out without authority, power, influence, or any combination of these three.

Please define these concepts for me.

There are many definitions of authority. I use sociologist Max Weber's definition: "the legal right to make certain decisions." It is independent of *what* the person knows and *who* he knows. It is independent of his personality. It is part of the position in the organization, and anyone who holds that job has the formal right to make the decisions associated with that position. It is the formal authority.

Now I'm going to eliminate the phrase "the right to make certain decisions" and substitute it with "the right to say yes." You continue.

...or no!

Wrong. You've made a common mistake. The word "or" is dangerous.

Why?

There are many organizations where people can say no but not yes to suggestions that lead to change. This can bureaucratize an organization. In a bureaucracy, you will find many managers who can say no but only infrequently have the authority, the legal right, to say yes to decisions that cause change. Only the person at the top has the right to say yes *and* no.

When organizations are young, founders can say yes *and* no. They have full authority; there is no question about where one needs to go for approval of a decision. As organizations grow and become too complicated for founders to manage alone, they have to delegate authority. Usually they hesitate to delegate the right to say yes for fear of losing control. As a result, they delegate only the right to say no. As organizations grow, the yes stays with the president. And so more and more layers of no–sayers separate the yes–sayer from where the action is. That's very dangerous, because authority to say only no prohibits change and bureaucratizes an organization. If authority is the right to make decisions about change, then authority should be the right to say yes *and* no. In this methodology, authority is defined as the right to say yes *and* no. If managers cannot say yes, neither should they be able to say no.

If your boss says no when you propose some sort of change, ask whether he or she is allowed to say yes. If your boss is not permitted to say yes, then ask who can. That person is really the only one who should be able to say no. That's how to keep an organization young and capable of dealing promptly with change.

What's next?

Next, I'm going to depict authority as a circle.

> *I get the idea. The circle also encloses space. The circle's bound-
> aries define the authority I have or, in other words, what decisions
> I am legally empowered to make. The space outside the circle
> represents the areas over which I have no authority.*

Now superimpose the circle of authority on the *(PAEI)* square of defined
responsibility. What do you get?

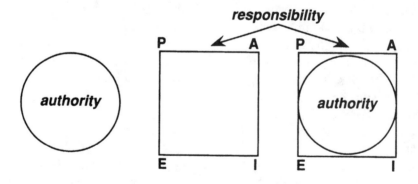

> *The square and the circle can never fully overlap. That means
> authority will never be equal to responsibility. But how can
> that be?*

I purposely depicted authority as a circle and responsibility as a square so that they would never equal each other. By definition then, you may have authority beyond your defined responsibility at times, and at other times you may have more responsibility than authority.

> *Most people would call this bad management. How can someone be responsible for something yet not have the necessary authority?*

I think differently. I believe it's good. It happens all the time in reality, and it should happen.

> *Good? Are you serious? If I have responsibility without the authority to carry out a task, how can I perform the task and be evaluated fairly?*

What I have given you so far is an optical illusion. Can you really take a responsibility and draw it as a square with distinct lines so that there is no question as to what you're responsible for and what you're not responsible for? Can you do that in reality?

> *Obviously not.*

Why not?

> *Because there is change. Whatever we decided yesterday might not be applicable today. Responsibility is "more or less."*

What about authority?

> *It's the same. It changes. You cannot delineate it perfectly. Its boundaries shift with time as people (bosses, employees, peers, situations) change.*

> *The square and the circle can never fully overlap. That means authority will never be equal to responsibility. But how can that be?*

Responsibility and authority would be better depicted like this.

When do you know *exactly* what you're responsible for and *exactly* what authority you have? When do you have both steady responsibility and authority such that you can stabilize and make them equal to each other?

Only when there is no change.

And when does that happen?

When you're dead.

Right. You are fully in control of your life only when you're dead. Being alive means not being fully in control. Sometimes you have more control than you need; sometimes you don't have enough. That's life. Not knowing your precise authority and responsibility in a constantly changing world is normal and even desirable.

Desirable? How do you figure that?

Because it means you are alive, and the more alive you are the more you run into situations where you are not in authority or control.

And how do I handle that?

Since authority cannot equal responsibility all the time, you will sometimes have responsibility without commensurate authority. What should you do then to carry out your responsibility?

Ask for the authority. Go and get it.

And if you have authority without responsibility?

Take on more responsibility.

Right. In a young company, 40 percent of the responsibility and authority is given, 60 percent is taken. In an older company, 60 percent is given, 40 percent is taken. And don't take these numbers literally, like an *(A)*. The day when one hundred percent of the authority and responsibility is given and none is taken, the organization is dead. That's why not knowing precisely your authority and responsibility is desirable. It means that the organization is young, alive and changing.

But how can managers function with this kind of uncertainty?

If you believe it's your responsibility, then it's your responsibility.

But I might invade someone else's territory. What if my responsibility overlaps with someone else's?

What is wrong with picking up the phone and saying, "We have a problem. Is it mine or yours?" How do you play doubles in tennis? Do you draw a chalk line down the middle of the court, saying, "This is your area, and this is mine." When the ball comes at high speed, do you wait until you're sure where it's going to land before deciding who is responsible for hitting it back? Obviously not. You *both* watch for the ball. Part of the area is yours, part of the area is your teammate's, and whose is the middle?

Ours!

So if the ball comes down the middle, you both might make a move. Therefore, you should watch the ball *and* each other.

But if we both make a move for the ball, that's not efficient, right?

Yes, but in order to be effective in hitting the ball, we might have to sacrifice some efficiency. Both of us may have to make a move for the ball, even if it's just our eyes that move.

Have you watched bureaucracies operate? To maximize efficiency they say, "This is your area. Don't step into anyone else's." Everyone has a precisely defined domain of responsibility so that no one wastes energy doing someone else's job. Very efficient. But what happens when things change? Say a problem develops in an area where it's not clear who is responsible. The ball has landed between two players, and neither is sure whose "ball" or problem it is. What does a bureaucracy usually do?

> *It appoints a third person to stand in the middle.*

Yes. Now there are two new areas with potential for uncertainty as to who is responsible. One year later what will the bureaucracy do?

> *It appoints two more people to cover the new uncertainties. Soon there will be a hundred areas where people overlap and feel uncertain about who is responsible. The court will be overrun with players.*

And by then nobody is playing tennis. They're watching each other instead of the ball. "Don't step over this line. This is my territory." "No! This is *my* territory!" It's called turf wars. Nobody even notices the ball unless it hits him or her smack between the eyes. Everyone is too busy protecting his domain.

> *You mean that in a bureaucracy people focus more on the how and who than on the what and why?*

Haven't you seen that in your experience? Bureaucracies are ineffective because they try to be too efficient in assigning *individual* responsibilities and eliminating uncertainties. Have you seen job descriptions in a bureaucratic organization? It would take a battery of lawyers to interpret them. Have you looked at their manuals? They contain pages and pages of *how* to do something rather than *why* to do it.

> *Sometimes when dealing with areas of overlapping responsibility, they appoint a committee. Bureaucracies have lots of committees. Isn't that a solution to the overlap issue?*

Maybe. But usually a committee doesn't feel responsible either.

But why doesn't the committee feel responsible? That was the purpose of forming the committee in the first place.

One reason is that in our culture if a person does not have exclusive authority, then he or she won't *feel* responsible. Since the individuals on a committee don't share authority, they don't have a sense of sharing responsibility either.

But why don't they share authority?

Because a bureaucracy has an *(A)* culture where people would rather be precisely wrong than approximately right. When responsibility, and thus authority, are not clearly delineated, it is politically less risky to create a new position or have a committee discuss it to death than to take initiative and exercise questionable authority.

You can see more clearly how *(A)s* act by comparing them to *(E)s*. *(A)s* ask permission. *(E)s* ask forgiveness. For *(A)s*, everything is forbidden unless expressly permitted. For *(E)s*, everything is permitted unless expressly forbidden.

In government it is this attention to precision and avoidance of risk that fosters bureaucratic growth. Some societies reinforce this risk avoidance for fear government may overstep its bounds. By limiting authority, society prevents government agencies from taking initiative.

But this could be fully justifiable. You don't want government officials overstepping their authority. That can endanger the control a society wishes to exercise on its public servants. Government officials are there to serve, not overrun, the people.

Good point. Do you know what the root of the word to *administer* is? It is "to serve." That's why we say public administration instead of public management. We use the terms "arts administration," "education administration" and "health administration." Public servants, as the name suggests, are supposed to serve the artists, teachers, medical personnel, and the people in general. They are there to facilitate, not manage.

We want public servants, as *(pAeI)s*, to stay within their defined responsibilities. The artists, teachers, and medical personnel are the *(PaEi)s*.

Then how do you keep public servants from becoming bureaucrats and bureaucratizing the organization?

They must share the authority and responsibility with the artists or scientists or whomever they serve. It's a complementary team.

Who performs the (E) role in government, then?

The politicians.

I can see why there is no love lost between the governmental machinery and the political machinery. It appears to be the typical (E) versus (A) conflict.

And integrating the political structure into the governmental structure is a difficult process. It can be done, and I have done it. But let's not digress anymore. Let's go back to your surprise when I recommended that authority not match responsibility exactly. I say that responsibility should equal authority, *more or less.*

But don't all management textbooks say just the opposite?

Yes they do, and I disagree. The parity they prescribe doesn't occur in the real world. Have you ever met a manager who claims to have all the authority he or she needs for their responsibility? Managers complain they don't have sufficient authority. In young companies authority is clear, and responsibilities are ambiguous. In aging companies responsibilities are clear, and authority is ambiguous. Only when an organization is in its Prime does authority equal responsibility, and both are functionally ambiguous.

And you say this is normal because both the square (responsibility) and the circle (authority) are changing. They always shift and rarely, if ever, fully overlap.

Yes, the relationship of authority to responsibility must be *more or less* rather than perfectly equal, because of the reality called CHANGE!

But how do you handle "more or less"? How do you handle the areas of uncertainty? The higher the rate of change, the higher the uncertainty, right? How do you handle uncertainty?

Through teamwork. If we have overlapping responsibilities, we should also have overlapping authority.

The greater the rate of change, the greater the level of uncertainty, which means the greater will be the degree of overlapping responsibility needed. This overlapping responsibility calls for greater overlapping authority. The greater the overlaps in authority and responsibility, the better the teamwork will have to be or, in a chronic change situation, bureaucracy will mushroom. Bottom line conclusion: the faster the rate of change, the better the teamwork has to be, or bureaucracy will mushroom.

You mean my success depends, to some degree, on others.

You are most vulnerable when you fight this reality and attempt to negate your interdependence. Just remember, the organization was born with interdependence, and this interdependence was tested when you all came upon a rock blocking your way, a rock none of you *alone* could lift. The organization was born when the need for interdependence was recognized. There is no organization and no management without interdependence. If you do not accept this, you can't manage.

What about power? What else do we have beyond authority?

Power is the capability, not the right, to punish and/or reward. If I can hurt you or make you happy, I have power over you.

And when does that happen?

If you need anything from me, I have power over you.

Okay.

Now, would you agree with me that to withhold expected rewards is a punishment?

Yes.

If you expect something from me and I deny it, I'm punishing you. I might respond, "I'm not punishing you. I'm just not giving you what you want." Well, that's a punishment, isn't it?

I've seen that happen in some bad marriages.

You want to punish people? Promise them something, then don't deliver it. They will be upset and hurt. You let them build expectations that were not met. And the way to punish yourself is to expect too much of yourself. When you can't deliver, you'll really come down hard on yourself. The road to Happiness does not go through Expectationsville.

Are you telling me then to be a vegetable, someone who wants nothing?

I didn't say to want nothing. Wanting is all right. Just don't expect it. The more ambitious you are, the more frustrated you become, and the harder you are on yourself and on others.

As far as organizations are concerned, you said that power is the capability to punish or reward, and that withholding expected rewards is equivalent to punishment.

Right. Power is the capability to grant or withhold expected rewards. Since you cannot lift the rock alone, you need the cooperation of others. And since there are many rocks on the path to the realization of any goal, whoever you need to assist you in lifting the rock (your responsibility) has power over you. Power is the *capability* to grant or withhold needed cooperation.

Let me see if I understand. If I could do the job by myself, there would be no organization because I would not need others. Since I can't carry out my responsibility alone, whoever I need has power over me.

The measure of their power is a function of how much you need them and how much of a monopoly they have over what you need. That's why falling in love or being infatuated with someone is an overpowering experience. We say, "I need you so much. I can't live without you. You're the only one for me." That situation can be extremely painful or gratifying, depending on the response.

So when am I totally free?

When you can say, "I don't need anybody for anything."

But you're going to tell me that will happen only when I'm dead!

Interestingly enough, that's the epitaph on the headstone of Nikos Kazantzakis, author of *Zorba the Greek:* "No more hope, no more fear. Finally free."

As long as you hope for or fear something, that thing has power over you. Being a member of a civilized society, living in a highly interdependent environment, means relying on others. Thus, the more civilized (developed) the society, the more powerless the individuals in it will feel. Whoever you need, for whatever reason, has power over you. They're as powerful as the importance you attach to whatever you need from them.

Now let me ask you a question. As a manager, where is the power?

Good question. Is it above, below, or beside you? Who do you need the most?

The power is above me. My boss has the most power.

You have confused power with authority. In the upper strata of the organization, there is more authority, not power. Maybe there is some authorized power, but raw power with no authority is in the hands of those you need most to accomplish your responsibility. Who are they?

The employees.

They *can* withhold cooperation without having the authority to do so. If they do, you can't carry out your responsibility. You will have difficulty lifting the rock of your managerial responsibility without them.

One time I was in the shipping department of a shoe factory talking to one of the workers. He took a liking to me and trusted me, so he said, "You know what we do sometimes when we get angry with the bosses? We take one shoe of one size, another shoe of another size, put them in the same box, and ship them out."

I visualized the strategic planners, consultants, and top executives working hard, making marketing and product differentiation decisions. Then here's this guy making minimum wage who's capable of ruining their whole strategy by not cooperating.

What is the value of a decision if the employees sabotage it? Uncooperative flight attendants can ruin an airline's multimillion–dollar advertising campaign just by being rude to customers. It's the people on the line who make a company flourish or die.

Many people believe the way to power is to climb the organizational ladder. They climb and bloody themselves as they fight their way up. Finally when they reach the top, exhausted, they find a sign saying, "It's down there." Many managers have to learn that the higher they go, the more they have to respect who is "down there." Because that's where their dreams and plans will be either fulfilled or dashed.

When does a military organization lose a war? When the generals have not been in the trenches for a long time. When they ignore the soldiers on the line.

What about influence? Is that important?

Influence is the capability, *not the right*, to make another person do something without using authority or power.

Give me an example.

What I'm doing right now, I hope, is influencing you. I have no authority to tell you what to do. I have no power to withhold future information or cooperation from you if you don't do what I am teaching here. I don't even know whether we will meet again. Thus if you do anything differently Monday morning in light of these conversations, it is because you have been persuaded. You believe in it because it makes sense to you.

When people take our input and make their own decisions based on this input, we have influenced them. When people are free to act of their own volition, they have been influenced. Anything other than that is not influence; rather it is a combination of power, authority, and/or influence.

But power, authority, and influence aren't separate. They are inter-related.

Absolutely. Let's look at the combinations. Let's look at authority, power and influence as circles that overlap.

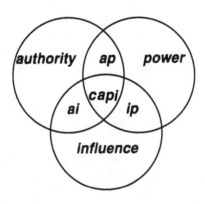

It's a Venn diagram, the type used in symbolic logic to show relation-ships between sets.

When authority and power overlap, what do you get? Authorized power. That is the *right* to punish and reward. For instance, when someone has the right to promote, to increase salaries, and to approve vacation time, he has authorized power.

When they're not overlapping, that's authority without power. What does that mean?

It means you have the right to tell someone what to do, but if he doesn't do it, you can't really do anything about it. You don't wish to stir up a hornets' nest. This might be the case, for instance, with a talented researcher in the company who insists on working differently from all other scientists. Be-cause she is valuable to you, you leave her alone even though you have the authority to order her to conform. The cost of using your authority might be higher than the long-term value. That's authority without effective power.

What about power without authority?

Power without authority occurs in situations in which you can withhold cooperation without being caught. Consider the difficulty of trying to catch the worker who put the wrong shoes in the box. If you can catch and punish such workers, then they don't have power. But if you can't catch them, they do have power. Another example is postal workers, who can easily misdirect the mail. You can't monitor every worker. As for salespeople on the road, you can't accompany them and control exactly what they do and how they do it. They have the effective capability to withhold cooperation if they want to. That's why we control salespeople mostly by results. If you try to control the process, it's often more expensive than it's worth. So you had better motivate them to do it right. This is where influence comes in.

What about the situation in which power and influence overlap?

I call this indirect power. If somebody tries to influence you, but you don't feel you have the freedom to decide, that person has indirect power. You read the influence as a threat, as power. Reading between the lines you realize that you had better do what the person says.

Give me an example.

A staff vice president from the corporate headquarters visits a factory and gives the production line some suggestions. This person has no authority to decide. He or she just "suggests." But the line is frightened by this executive from headquarters and follows the suggestion. When the decision results in disaster, the line says, "Corporate staff told me to do it." The vice president will respond, "Not true. I only suggested." The line feels no responsibility, since it feels it was threatened into submission. The corporate person feels no responsibility, because he or she didn't authorize the line to do anything. After all, this person had no authority to decide. The end result? No one takes responsibility for what happened.

What about when influence overlaps authority?

I call it influencing authority. That's what the late business author and statesman Chester Barnard called "authority by acceptance" or "professional authority." The person with authority has the right to say what to do, but can also convince people of the validity of what he or she says. That's when we say, "My boss is an authority on the subject. I think she's right and I'm going to do what she says." That's accepted authority.

Where authority, power and influence overlap, you get a new combination. I call this *capi*. The letter c stands for "coalesced." You have coalesced authority, power and influence. You have the authority to tell people what to do, you have the power to punish or reward them, and you can also influence them as to the validity of what you want done. There is no reason, when you have *capi*, why people would not follow your decisions. You have the legal right to decide, they know you have the power to punish and reward, and they're persuaded by the content of your decision that it is the right one. In this case, you have control.

I like that.

Now, my friend, it is time to rest. We have learned that to implement decisions we have to define them well first, and that means...

That all (PAEI) imperatives should be fully expressed.

And that means...

What, how, when and who

And...

What not, how not, when not and who not.

And in order to carry out this well–defined decision, we need authority, power and influence...

Or any combination of the three.

Next time, let's discuss how to predict the efficiency with which a decision will be implemented.

Conversation 8

Predicting the Efficiency of Implementing Decisions

Now where did we finish our last conversation?

Let me summarize. I have a well–defined (PAEI) decision, a square of responsibility, and I understand authority, power, influence, and their combinations. You promised to tell me how to predict efficient implementation.

Let's superimpose authority, power, and influence, as depicted in our diagram, on the square of responsibility and see what happens. We'll take three situations.

In this first case, managers have authority, power, and influence, or any combination of them, to carry out their responsibility. But the *capi* component, the core of the diagram where the three overlap, does not cover their responsibility. It is too small. What does this mean?

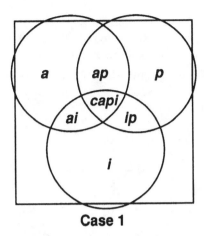

Case 1

These managers have enough authority and/or power and/or influence to carry out their responsibility, but don't have control (capi) over all of their responsibilities.

Right. Can people who have sufficient authority and/or power and/or influence in any combination, carry out their responsibility? Can they be effective? Will they be able to implement their decisions?

They will be the type of managers who juggle. Over some parts of their responsibility, they have only authority. They will have to decide and then hope their decision is carried out. On other parts where they have no authority but where they do have power, they say to those whose help they need, "Help me out and I'll help you later." In the third part of their responsibility, they have only influence. They have to convince others to help.

They control only a very small part of their responsibility where they have capi. In that area, they make decisions and things get done because they have authority and power and influence.

But the circles do not fully cover the square. In some areas of responsibility, these managers have no authority, no power, and no influence.

That's normal, because of change. The square and the circles "move." They are rarely equal anyway.

When responsibility is larger than authority or authority is larger than responsibility, the person will have to take responsibility and/or authority. We'll discuss later how to do this. Now let's proceed to the second case, in which the authority, power, and influence circles do not overlap, although they cover, more or less, the square of responsibility. There is no *capi*. How does that look graphically?

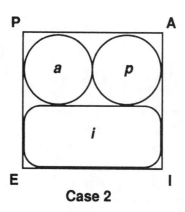

Case 2

Can managers implement their decisions in this case? Can they be responsible?

It's going to be more difficult this time.

Why?

Because authority without power isn't worth much. What can one do with authority and no power?

How about power without authority?

Power without authority is very dangerous. It works in the short run but backfires sooner or later because it is not legitimized.

And just influence?

Influence without authority and power works, but it takes a long time to build influence.

So what do managers do in the short run?

They can be effective, but I bet they won't sleep very well. They'll spend sleepless nights thinking of ways to enforce their decisions.

Now let's take the third case. The three circles overlap completely so that you have total *capi*, and it almost covers the square.

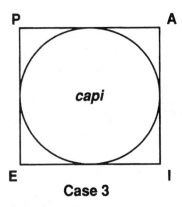

Case 3

How do you read this diagram?

For every part of their responsibility, managers have authority, power, and influence reinforcing each other.

Can they implement their decisions now?

You bet! They have the right to decide and can back that right with influence and power, both of which are legitimized and in their possession.

Managers in this situation decide, and it happens. Let's look again at these three cases.

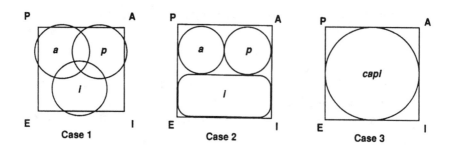

Case 1   Case 2   Case 3

Can the managers in each of these three cases carry out their responsibilities?

> *Yes, as long as they have authority and/or power and/or influence. As long as the circles cover the square, more or less, they can get their managerial job done.*

Which means they are equally effective in each case. But are they equally efficient? Who sleeps best at night? All they have to do is decide and it will get done.

> *The managers in the third case!*

Right. They have full *capi*, or full authority, power, and influence over their responsibilities. They decide and they can sleep. Who is the least efficient? Who sleeps the least at night?

> *The managers with zero capi.*

You have just discovered a very important concept: managerial or leadership efficiency. It can be measured by the energy managers have to expend in order to implement their decisions.

Managerial effectiveness is a function of authority and/or power and/or influence in relation to responsibilities. Managers are effective when they have sufficient authority and/or power and/or influence for their responsibility. I call this total managing energy *authorance*, symbolized by $A\Sigma$, which is the mathematical notation for the sum or totality of authorance. Authorance is equal to authority, power, and influence, the union of authority and power, the union of authority and influence, the union of influence and power and *capi*. In mathematical symbols, it can be written like this:

$$A\Sigma = a + p + i + \mu ap + \mu ai + \mu ip + \mu api$$

Capi, on the other hand, is just the core of the Venn diagram, where authority, power, and influence overlap.

$$capi = \mu api$$

Managerial effectiveness $= f \left\{ \text{authorance / responsibility} \right\}$

You can be effective as a manager as long as you have sufficient authorance to carry out your responsibilities. Managerial efficiency is a function of the amount of *capi* held by the managers out of the total authorance they have. The more capi, the less begging and praying they have to do.

Managerial efficiency $= f \left\{ \textit{capi} \text{ / authorance} \right\}$

I believe I understand. All managers need in order to implement decisions effectively and efficiently is full capi over their responsibilities. It means they should have all the authority, power and influence they need to carry out their decisions.

Right. But how often do you find people with full *capi*, full control over their responsibilities? The situation may exist in a dictatorship, but only for a short while.

Why?

Imagine having complete authority, power, and influence. Which source of managerial energy (authorance) would you be inclined to use most? Which is the most efficient?

Power! I can see that with children. When I don't have the time to persuade them to do something, I threaten punishment.

That's why "power corrupts and absolute power corrupts absolutely." Power gives instant results, but over time higher and higher doses are necessary to achieve the same impact. It's like a drug.

Power corrupts because it is effective and easy to use. When you have all the power you need to carry out your responsibilities, there is a good chance you will be tempted to use it exclusively. If you do, it will undermine your influence and diminish your authority. The effectiveness of power decreases the more you use it. Eventually, you lose your power because there is a limit on how much you can punish. Full *capi* is very rare, and even then it is not a stable situation.

But if no single individual has capi on every responsibility and every time, does it mean that all decisions will be inefficiently implemented? No. I, see. This is the same conclusion we reached about (PAEI). Although we need full capi, no one person has it alone. For full capi, again, we need a team.

Back to teamwork. But this time, we need the team not to make a decision, but to implement one. If managers do not have *capi* for the totality of their responsibilities, they need to seek the cooperation of others. They must take into account the interests of the people whose cooperation they're seeking, those who have power and/or influence.

That makes sense. But people can't manage through a team all the time. Do managers call a meeting every time they want to change anything? That would paralyze a company. What do normal managers do?

Good question. Let's see if we can figure out the answer. Which of the three cases is the most frequently encountered?

The first, I think, in which a manager has capi over some responsibilities; authority, power, or influence over other responsibilities; and a combination or none of them over the remainder.

We have to learn how to increase the efficiency of what we do under *normal* circumstances. Stop dreaming of becoming a dictator with full *capi* over everything. Too many managers in the dead of night mumble to themselves, "Oh, if only I had all the power I need. If only we could destroy the unions. If only people really had to work for their money! Then I wouldn't have any problems. Things would happen then!" I have news for such managers. In the long run, dictatorial powers will not give them control. They have to stop dreaming of total power and dictatorial management. Instead, they must learn how to work under normal circumstances in which they don't have all the power and authority and influence they need.

Hmm. How do they do that?

Assume that the first case is a dart board, like the one that's frequently cited in jokes about security analysts. When they don't know what to do, they throw a dart at the board where different areas are labeled "buy," "sell," "sell short," "jump out the window" and so on. Let's play the same dart game on our circles and square and see what happens. A problem comes to you, usually through the mail, the telephone, or the door. How are you going to solve it? Take a dart and throw it at the board. Let's assume that the dart hits far away from the square, as I've drawn it here. What should you do?

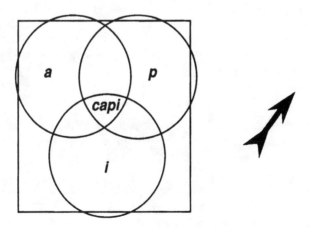

Obviously, this problem is not my responsibility.

Right. Don't be like the Lone Rangers, who assume everything is their responsibility. They're like managerial vacuum cleaners. They yell at their subordinates, "What are you doing with that problem? Put it on my desk." By the time they finish walking through the company, they have sucked in all its problems for themselves.

Not everything is your problem. If it is not in your square, say, "It's not my responsibility. Go to Jack or Bill or Donna." In an organization, we must have distinct areas of responsibility. Note, however, that you are responsible to take the problem to Jack, Bill, or Donna. Don't ignore the problem just because it doesn't fall into your square of responsibility.

If you are the president, you decide the boundaries of your square by including or excluding areas of responsibility for yourself. You feel responsible for everything, although you don't have to do it all personally. You care for everything as if it is all your responsibility.

> *But that's true also for sociopolitical activists who are socially conscious and fight for what they believe in. They will behave the same way even though they're not the president.*

Good point. That's why in a democracy, every citizen is not only a possible candidate for the presidency, but every citizen should think like a president. Every citizen should care for the totality and be involved in caring for it.

> *The same holds true for a well-managed organization. Every employee should think like a manager. Every manager should feel like the employee feels.*

The Problem
Now let's throw the next dart. This time, the dart hits smack in the bull's–eye of your square, in *capi*. Is that problem your responsibility?

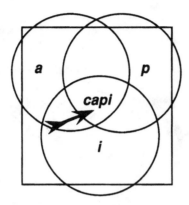

Yes. It is in my square of responsibility.

You have authority, power, and influence? You have *capi?*

Yes.

What should you do about this problem? It's your responsibility. You have all the necessary authority, power, and influence. What should you do?

Decide! Make a decision and carry it through.

Right. In California they would say, "It's your problem!" Don't call a meeting. There's no need. If you do call one, it's to inform others of your decision. If they don't like it, you'll accept resignations Monday morning. We don't need participative management here. It's your responsibility and you're in control. Do it!

Now throw the next dart. This time, as you can see, it falls inside the square and in the authority circle, which means it's your responsibility, but you have only authority over the matter. You have no power and no influence. Are you responsible?

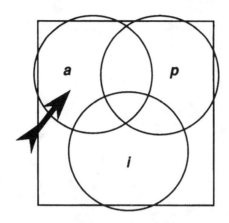

Yes.

But you only have authority. What should you do without power or influence?

Now is the time to call a meeting.

Right. But why?

Because authority without power and influence won't take me far.

In fact, if you only have authority, you are in a "managerial overdraft."

What?

Let me show you, because it's too important to miss.

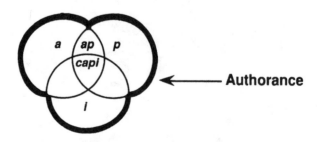

Let's look at the managerial task a mother has in trying to convince her child to eat spinach. First, she says, "Eat. It's good for you. Popeye eats spinach. Look how strong he is. If you eat spinach, you'll be strong like Popeye."

Where is she on the diagram? What part of authorance is she using?

Influence.

Right. But the kid says, "Noooo! I hate spinach." So the mother tries again, saying, "When Daddy comes home, I'm going to tell him you were a good boy. And if you eat your spinach, he'll take you to the zoo." She has moved out of influence and is now using...

Influencing power.

Yes, by referring to the potential rewards or dangers, she is using influencing power. But still the kid refuses to eat.

If the mother gets very upset and punishes the child, what is she using?

Authorized power.

But if the husband comes home and says, "What have you done? What are you punishing the kid for? If he doesn't want to eat spinach, he doesn't have to."

Then she was using unauthorized power.

This is likely to happen in modern families in which parents share authority. No one can claim exclusive authority.

The kids still refuses to eat spinach, and he's crying. So the mother starts crying, too. "You never listen to me. You never do what your mother tells you to. What's wrong with you? Listen to me. *I'm your mother!*"

Now, she's using authority. But doesn't the child already know that she's his mother?

Right. That's the point! The day you have to remind people of your authority when it should be obvious is the day you are in managerial overdraft.

The day you tell your employees, "Do it because I'm your boss," what are you reminding them of? Don't they know you're the boss? If you have to remind them of such an obvious fact, you're in trouble. When somebody says, "But I'm your husband," or "I'm your wife," he or she is saying something equally obvious. It means that all sources of authorance, of managerial energy, have been exhausted. The person is down to the last gasp of breath. This is very dangerous because certain facts should never be spoken. After you say them aloud, you're left with nothing.

So authority in itself is very weak unless it's backed with power and influence. And you probably can't use authority alone more than once or twice. If you plead repeatedly with your children, "But I'm your parent," they eventually might say, "So what!" In that case there is really nothing else you can do.

What should you do then, if you have only authority?

Call a meeting.

Why?

To coalesce power and influence.

And whom should you have at the meeting?

Those people with the power to sabotage my solution, the people whose cooperation I need and the people who wield influence. They can convince other people.

I don't call this situation a "problem." I call it a "pre–problem," because you cannot solve *the* problem until you solve the pre–problem.

What is the pre–problem?

The Pre–Problem
When you call a meeting, you can't be certain everyone will come. If they come, you can't be certain they'll cooperate. You might call a meeting, and people won't come because they don't work for you. Maybe they do work for you, but the trade union doesn't want them to come for fear they'll be co–opted. Or maybe they don't trust you, or don't respect you, or think it is

not their problem... whatever. And even if they do they will behave as if they weren't there.

So what do I do?

You have to solve the pre–problem first. You have to persuade them to cooperate. You have to solve the pre–problem of creating a cooperative environment before you can solve the problem for which you need their cooperation.

How do I do that?

A joke will illustrate the point. A hen and a pig were very good friends. One day the hen said, "We get along so well, why don't we start a business together?" The pig answered, "Good idea. What do you have in mind?" The hen said, "Well, I've studied the current market conditions and looked for opportunities in which we would have synergistic capabilities. I concluded we should start a restaurant chain serving... ham and eggs." The pig looked at the hen and said, "It's a great idea, but what is a mere contribution for you is a total commitment from me."

Many decisions are for the good of an organization, but they're not in the interests of the people necessary to implement the decisions.

Where are you leading?

Each component—authority, power and influence—reflects the different self interests of the different people involved. Authority usually reflects the self–interests of management. They have the authority that flows from the stockholders to the board of directors to management. They act "in the name of." Management possesses the legal authority.

Who has the power?

The subordinates. Labor, unionized or not.

Aha. And if they're unionized, it's authorized power.

The employees have power, and their horizon is different from management's. Management wants to make the company grow, to get the biggest return on investment. They want the organization to be strong in the long run. And management is rewarded through stock options and bonuses. What is labor interested in? In the short run, in money, fringe benefits, etc.

Why? That doesn't seem very loyal.

It's normal though, and to be expected. Employees don't know if they will stay with the organization for the long run to benefit from long range plans. They don't participate in making them. Frequently, they don't even know what they are. Frequently, those long–term plans exclude them. They might be fired on short notice. They have no control, no stock options. For management could benefit in the long run with profit sharing and golden parachutes. Each group is naturally interested in what it can benefit from. What is so surprising about that? The United States was built on the notion of self–interest and the pursuit of happiness.

Now I understand why Japanese workers are more committed and supportive of change. The company is committed to them for the long run, and through profit sharing, the workers will benefit from their cooperation. I didn't think about that.

Yes, but be careful. Some countries, like Sweden, have long term employment and participatory management, but it produces different results. It depends on *how* you conduct such management. The Japanese have participatory management and lifetime employment as a manifestation of their *(I)* culture. The moment you do it by law, as in Sweden, it is...

(A).

Right. By law you can't fire, and by law you must have participatory management.

Will that have an impact on the (E) role?

Absolutely. In Yugoslavia, for instance, the government also forced participatory management by law, by *(A)*. As a result, the economy virtually collapsed. The *(E)* and then necessarily the *(P)* fell apart. With the (E)ntrepreneur role suffocating, (P)roductivity suffered tremendously.

When (P) goes down and the economic conditions worsen, (I) can go down too. People talk against each other and look for a scapegoat. They have a political mess in addition to an economic one.

Another example is Sweden, where they tried to *(A)* the *(E)* factor.

How?

By law, people have to save and invest part of their income.

People must be hiding their income then.

I believe so. As their *(A)* mushrooms and strangles *(E)*, it will eventually kill *(P)*, too. In Swedish there is no direct translation of the word *entrepreneur*. They had a word 400 years ago, but the word died out! And if the word died...

So did the concept.

Yes, but I think we have digressed enough. We were discussing how people with authority and power have different interests.

Who has influence in an organization?

Influence is usually represented by the technocrats, staff people and professionals. What are they interested in? The biggest R&D budget, the most professional exposure, and the most liberal research capabilities.

I've noticed that with computer professionals. They switch companies at the drop of a hat if they're offered better computers elsewhere. The same with academicians. Their loyalty is to their field of knowledge, not to the organization that employs them.

Exactly. Each component of *capi* reflects a different self–interest. If you want to solve a pre–problem, what do you have to do? Think about the common interest and how to create a win–win climate. Think about why the people you need should come and solve the problem together. The mistake you might make is to call a meeting and say, "Ladies and gentlemen, *we* have a problem and *my* solution is..." They're going to think, "If *we* have a problem, why should we accept *your* solution?"

What you should say is, *"We* share a problem. *I* have a problem, and *you* have a problem. Let me tell you how I believe we share the problem. I have a suggestion for a solution, but I'd like to hear what *you* think so we can arrive at *our* solution. We have common interests here. We're in this boat together!"

> *Several years ago, when Miguel de la Madrid was running for President of Mexico, he had a slogan, "La solucion somos todos," which means, "The solution is all of us." According to your theory, if the solution is all the Mexican people, then the problem is all the Mexican people too.*

Which includes Mr. de la Madrid and his government. After his term expired, they accused him of being a major problem for Mexico. The people *alone* are not the problem and the government *alone* is not the solution. Both have to accept responsibility for being the problem and for finding the solution. Managers sometimes ask their employees, "Are you part of the solution or part of the problem?" This is an artificial distinction. A person should not be part of the solution if he isn't part of the problem; but if he is part of the problem, he had better be part of the solution.

> *Give me a business example.*

America is accused of having low productivity. It probably has one of the lowest rates of increase in productivity among industrial nations. Is that a problem?

> *Sure.*

Okay. Is it within management's square of responsibility to increase productivity?

> *Sure!*

Now let me ask you: Is it a problem, or a pre–problem?

It's a problem for management if management has all the author-
ity, power and, influence needed to increase productivity. But man-
agement does not have all the necessary managerial energy to solve
the problem. There are unions and other interested parties that
wield power and influence. All that management has is authority.
I've got it. It's a pre–problem.

Right, and if it's a pre–problem, authority needs to coalesce with power and
influence. That means productivity is not going to increase in the United
States until management and labor learn to work together. Productivity is
not a technological problem. It is a political–philosophical problem reflect-
ing political values. The United States possesses excellent technology. Thus
lack of technology is not what is causing low productivity. And American
workers as individuals are no less dedicated than the Japanese. The evi-
dence is seen in how well they work under Japanese management. Productivity is a political problem between two power centers: management and
labor. Do you know one of the reasons Japan and Germany are beating the
United States economically? They buy the technology from the United
States; then their management and labor cooperate and use the technology
to outshine American performance. American manufacturing is steeped in
the concept of adversarial relations between firms and *within* the firm.
Pluralism is breaking down businesses, even families. We are carrying
individualism too far. We prefer to fight one another rather than unite
against foreign competition.

The United States, then, will not improve its productivity until it
works out the antagonistic relationship between management
and labor.

America negates the rights of labor in decision making just as the Commu-
nists negated the rights of private ownership in the creation of value. This is
a major mistake. The Soviet Union's President Mikhail Gorbachev needs
to legitimize private ownership, a revolution in communist thinking. We
need a similar revolution in ours. We need to legitimize the right of labor to
manage and accept responsibility with (not against) management. Low
productivity is a pre–problem, not a problem. We are in denial by saying,
"Management should solve it." Management can't solve it *alone!*

You have to call a meeting when you have a pre–problem. You have
to ask yourself, "How can I present it as our shared problem and create a

climate in which we can arrive at a joint solution?"

What if you can get rid of some people and then seize power? Wouldn't that convert a pre-problem into a problem?

You may commit organizational suicide trying to do that. The problem might not warrant such a sacrifice. In fact, you might hurt yourself more than those who oppose you. If you can't fight them, it might be better to join them.

The Pre–Pre–Problem

What happens when the dart falls into the influence circle? It's my responsibility, but I have neither authority nor power, only influence.

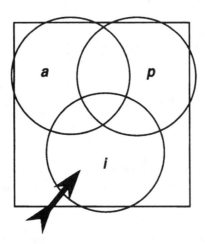

This happens in many organizations. The people above you have the authority, the people below you have the power, and you are in the middle. You have only influence to carry out your responsibility.

Sounds like good cause for tension and high blood pressure.

Some people simply relax and say, "The hell with it. It's not my responsibility. If I don't have the authority or power, I can't be responsible." So they shrink the area for which they feel responsible. That's why, in many organizations, there are responsibilities for which nobody takes responsibility. Consequently, the organization is ineffective and the clients suffer.

But assuming you want to do the job, what do you have to do?

You have to use your influence. I call this situation a pre–pre–problem. In this situation you have to convince the people with authority to call a meeting of those with power and influence. The total group can then coalesce *capi* to solve the problem for which you are responsible.

This seems very difficult.

Not once you learn the necessary skills. You have to communicate to different people in their own language. The way you communicate with a *(P)* is different from the way you communicate with an *(A)*, an *(E)*, or an *(I)*. Each of them speaks a different language. Another conversation between us is necessary to discuss these different languages, but let me give you some pointers.

For instance, big *(A)s*, whether Bureaucrats or Administrators, usually do not like to talk about opportunities. For them, every opportunity is a problem. They always think about the repercussions of suggested ideas. Arsonists or Entrepreneurs usually hate to talk about problems. "I pay *you* to solve problems," they say. They prefer to talk about opportunities. Thus an opportunity for an *(E)*, however, is a problem for an *(A)*. That's why they usually don't like each other.

Interestingly, the words "opportunity" and "problem" truly mean the same thing. In Chinese, both words have the same character. Whether something is a problem or an opportunity depends upon who is looking at it.

Your attitude defines whether something is a problem or an opportunity. If you solve the problem, you become stronger and better as a result. So it was really an opportunity. On the other hand, if you miss an opportunity by doing nothing while your competitor exploits it, that could be a problem for you.

That's why I have translated literally the Chinese word into English as "opporthreat." It describes a situation that could be an opportunity or a problem. It is whatever you make of it. "Opporthreat" is a neutral word while the words "problem" and "opportunity" are charged with emotion.

Here's another example about differences in style. When *(E)*s disagree with ideas, they're usually very vocal about it. They continuously talk and think out loud. Because of this, they dislike being alone. They're so talkative and creative you can hardly finish telling them a joke. If you start one, it will remind them of a different one. They'll even interrupt your punch line. They're very expressive. If they disagree, they make themselves heard. For them, silence means agreement.

> *The Jewish people, who are known for their strong (E) traits, have a Hebrew expression, "Shtika ke hodaya." "Silence is agreement." With (A)s, it's the opposite. They are quiet when they disagree. Look at the Scandinavians or British. When they disagree, they just freeze and look at you!*

That can cause tremendous miscommunication. Just imagine an *(E)* talking to an *(A)*. The *(E)* talks, talks talks, while the *(A)* doesn't say a word. When the *(E)* leaves, she'll think, "Fantastic! He's sold." Meanwhile the *(A)* is thinking, "She's crazy. She's going to destroy us. Her idea will never work." Sometime later, the *(E)* will ask the *(A)*, "What happened to the idea we agreed about?"

The *(A)* will respond, "Agreed about? I thought the idea would have been a disaster."

"But you didn't say a word," says the *(E)*, who now has one more reason not to trust the *(A)*. They obviously miscommunicated.

This is helpful!

Let me give you a third example of how different *(PAEI)* styles speak different languages. When *(A)*s don't know what's going on, and you ask them whether something can or cannot be done, they are inclined to say "no". Then you explain. They still say "no", because they still don't understand it fully. So you keep explaining, and finally, when they are sure they fully understand it—and that happens only when they realize that there is no risk involved—they'll say "yes".

So?

This means that for *(A)s*, "no" does not mean no; "no" means maybe. You have to continue interpreting the "no" as maybe until they fully understand you. Then they'll say, "Okay, I see what you mean. Yes."

Of course you realize that for *(A)s*, "yes" means yes. For them to say "yes" is like giving birth. They really suffer to say "yes", but once they do you can depend on it.

What about (E)s?

For (E)ntrepreneurs or Arsonists, it is just the opposite: "yes" means maybe. If you ask them, "Can we do that?" and it looks interesting, they may say, "Why not?" But this attitude lasts only as long as you do not intend to act. Talk is fine. They'll say, "Sure! Tell me more," until they understand it, and they understand it only when the time comes to act. Then they say, "What? That? No! You can't do that." For *(E)s*, "yes" means maybe and "no" is definite. If they say "no" and you assume the matter is still open for discussion, you'll be in trouble when you bring it up again.

That's why *(A)s* and *(E)s* misunderstand each other. *(A)s* hear "yes" from *(E)s* and move ahead. Then the *(E)s* change their mind, driving the *(A)s* crazy. "You said yes. Didn't you say yes?" The *(E)s* answer, "Well, I was just thinking out loud. I said yes with an upward inflection, not with a downward inflection."

It's the same in reverse. It drives *(E)s* mad to hear "no" from *(A)s*. "How can you say no? You don't know what we're talking about. I haven't finished speaking and you're already saying no." But the *(A)* didn't mean no; he meant maybe.

Now, for whom is "yes" really yes, and "no" really no? There is no confusion.

The (P)s.

And for whom does "yes" mean maybe and they avoid saying "no"?

The (I)s.

A chart of these tendencies would look like this.

meant / said	P	A	E	I
Yes	yes	yes	maybe	maybe
No	no	maybe	no	maybe

If you want to solve a problem when you have only influence, you have to know the different languages of the people with whom you are trying to communicate. If you don't, you'll miscommunicate. The rule is, "Don't treat them as if they were you." Usually we speak to others as if we were speaking to ourselves, then get upset when other people don't understand us. The trick is to speak to people in the language they understand.

This has been a long conversation. Would you please summarize for me?

Okay. Here we go.

In order to implement a decision, the decision must be well defined. What, how, why, when, and who must be established. Then you must have the authority, power, and influence to carry it through. Depending on whether you have *capi,* or just authority, or just influence, or just power, or a combination of the components of authorance, you have to develop a strategy for implementation. Are you starting with a problem, pre–problem or pre–pre–problem? If it is a pre–pre–problem you have to use influence by persuading in the style the listener understands. If you have only authority it is a pre–problem. You have to know how to create a win–win climate by searching for the common interest. Then you together can arrive at a conclusion you all support. If you have *capi,* it's your problem and you have to learn how to use *capi,* not abuse it; if you use only the power component of *capi,* it will eventually backfire.

If you have *capi*, you can be a technician. You have to know how to make the right decision, how to communicate, inspect and implement. If you have only authority, you have to be a politician. You have to create a win–win climate in which everyone is "in this together." If you have only influence, you have to be a practicing street psychologist. You have to know how to communicate with people in a language they understand.

You mean to say that a good manager, leader, or parent should be a technician, politician, and a practicing psychologist?

Yes. You need all three. Too many people say, "I love to manage. It's people I can't stand," or "I hate politics." All they want to do is make good decisions, and that's it. They want to be management technicians and not worry about selling their decisions. They don't wish to deal with people's unique interests and communication styles. They feel ill at ease when they have to solicit other people's cooperation. I have news for them—bad news. There are only a few cases in which a manager has *capi* and can afford the luxury of being a technician. Most of the time a person does not have full *capi* over all of his responsibility and thus needs to coalesce it.

Efficiency of implementation depends on how much *capi* can be coalesced for the task and how much cooperation can be secured for accomplishing the responsibility from people necessary for the implementation. For that, a person must be a technician, politician and psychologist.

Thank you very much. Can we continue some other time?

Of course. Let's add what we've discussed to our diagram before we go.

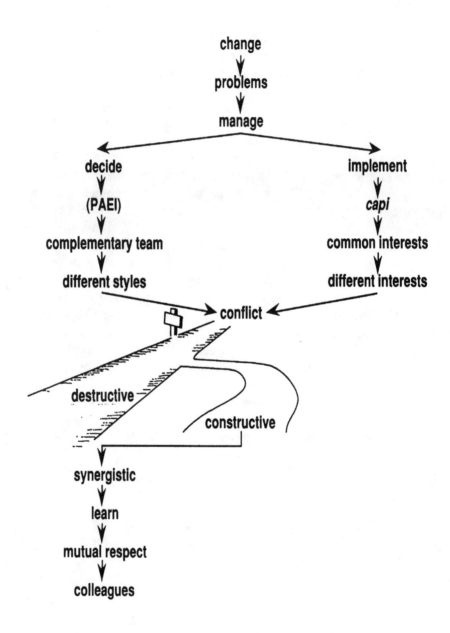

Conversation 9

What Makes the Wheels Turn

Just to be sure we understand each other, would you like to summarize what we've discussed so far?

So far we've said that to manage anything, whether it's our personal life, family life, business, or society, we must make good decisions and implement them using minimum energy and resources. This is how we need to deal with change, which is inevitable. So, how well we manage depends on how good our decisions are and how efficiently we implement them.

We've discovered that a good decision requires four imperatives, which you call roles. They are the (P) role, to (P)erform a needed service; the (A) role, to (A)dminister the service; the (E)ntrepreneurial role, to position for the changing future; and the (I) role, to (I)ntegrate the organization. These roles are necessary to make organizations effective and efficient in the short and long run.

Since no individual can be a perfect (PAEI), we need a complementary team. In a complementary team, however, there will necessarily be conflict.

149

To make the conflict constructive, we need to learn from each other's disagreements. For this to occur we need mutual respect.

To predict whether a decision will be a good one, we have to check whether it was devised by a complementary (PAEI) team that worked with mutual respect.

To implement decisions, we need capi: coalesced authority, power, and influence. We need to build a coalition of the different interests of the different people necessary to implement the decision. Implementation is always faster if propelled by self interest.

Who are the people involved? First, those who have the legal authority to approve a decision. Second, those who will carry out the decision in the field, who have the power to cooperate or not. Third, the people with influence, the ones with the technical and professional knowledge about the decision. Since they too have self–interests, their information will be biased and must be aligned with the biases of those with authority and power. We need to create common interests if we want to have the decision effectively implemented.

Good summary?

This is all well and good, but something has been bothering me since our last conversation. How did the myth of the perfect (PAEI) manager come about in management theory? It seems like a fundamental error.

The mistake lies in the way management theory is researched. The best characteristics of many different people are chosen to create a model. But such a model is really just a fanciful collage that cannot and does not exist. We are all human beings with strengths *and* weaknesses. None of us are perfect.

Another reason is that management theory was first developed in the United States where the culture is individualistic. Naturally, they personalized the whole process of management into one individual, called *the* Manager or *the* Leader.

But the U.S. also encourages entrepreneurship, an individual activity of considerable benefit to the nation and the individual.

Yes, but for *starting* companies, not for keeping them young and growing. For that you need a system such as the one in Japan that nourishes people.

The Japanese, unlike the Chinese, are not known as individual entrepreneurs, and yet look at the success of their system of cooperative entrepreneurship.

So the perfect (PAEI) manager does not exist?

Right. And it is dangerous to try to develop one.

Are you referring to business school graduates who believe they have all the answers?

If they earned straight A's from a leading school, they're especially dangerous. They might believe they're faultless. They might be arrogant, uncommunicative and very difficult to work with. I know a few of these people myself. They are not trained to ask for input from those that complement them so that they can make good decisions. They also received no training to help them unite people with different interests, even though they need the cooperation of those people to carry out decisions. The implementation process is also a source of conflict. We need to examine it as well.

We've said that in order to implement decisions efficiently we need a commonality of interests between authority, power and influence: a win–win climate. But that's more easily said than done. People have different interests. The idea of a win–win climate is wonderful, but how many lasting win–win climates can you create? Win–win situations don't always happen in families. Why should it happen in an impersonal organization?

So what do we do? The conflict of interests means that my needs are different from yours. What requires a mere contribution from you may require a total commitment from me. I may not want to do what is mainly in your interest.

That's how conflict can become destructive. Those who have the authority to decide can be undermined by those with power. They can make a sham out of decisions simply by not implementing them properly, claiming they did not understand them. They can undermine decisions to protect their interests. In the same way, those with authority may make decisions clearly in their interest at the expense of the interests of those with power. Whenever there are diverse interests among those who are needed to implement a decision, the political process of securing implementation can be lengthy and expensive. It may demand too much managerial energy.

So there are actually two sources of conflict. One is miscommunication because we speak different (PAEI) languages. The other is divergent interests, which lead to lack of cooperation.

Right. Either we don't understand each other or we don't share the same interests.

We solved the problem of conflicts that stem from the differences in decision–making styles. These differences can be synergistic when mutual respect creates a learning environment. But how do we make conflict constructive when we're working with divergent interests?

First, accept reality. Don't resist it. Only then can you harness it. Notice I said you have to *harness* conflict, not resolve it. Resolving conflict means fighting it. Don't try to fight it. Don't try to eliminate it. Make it functional. Make it work for you.

But having a win–win climate all the time is utopian. You just said that yourself.

Yes. The people involved in implementation realize that a win–win climate does not occur in the short run, but it's possible for them to see it *will* exist in the long run. This sort of long–term belief is the basis of many good marriages. Once there is commitment for the long run, one partner will give in today and the other will give in another time. It evens out over time.

You mean you have to start with commitment?

Absolutely. No ifs, ands or buts.

It still sounds utopian. If I give in to overcome a short–term conflict of interests, I must trust that the winning party will reciprocate in the future. I must trust that my sacrifice in the short run will be good for me in the long run. If I don't trust the people with whom I have a conflict of interests, why should I believe they will cooper-

ate over the long run? If I don't believe they'll cooperate later, why should I cooperate now?

Obviously, you won't give in at all unless you believe the favor will be returned. Thus to implement decisions, mutual respect is not enough. We must also have...

Mutual trust.

That's right. For implementation we need some common interests based on mutual trust. We have to trust that over the long run we will both benefit. Only then will we be willing to cooperate in the short run in spite of the short–run conflicts of interest.

Wait. I think I can predict whether that decision in the envelope will be implemented.

Yes...

First I should ask, "Who is needed for implementation? Could we get the people needed for capi together?"

And then?

"Do they trust each other?"

Yes, and this is the result of friendship and love.

Friendship and love? That sounds too easy.

I agree. These words have been used so much they either have too many meanings or no meaning at all. Let me talk about love first. Now, when I say love I don't mean passion or sexual infatuation. I'm talking about the love a parent feels for a child.

Look at the human body. It's completely integrated through the nervous system. If my finger is broken, I'll probably cry. But why are my eyes crying when it's my finger that's broken? Because the finger and the eye are part of a whole. My whole body aches because the pieces belong to each other. There is a totality, an interdependence.

Now suppose my son's finger is broken. Do I hurt? Yes, a lot. But it's not my finger, so why do I hurt? Because I feel for my son.

That's what you mean by the word love?

Love means belonging to one another. It doesn't have to be physical. It has more to do with a belonging to and caring for one another so that whatever happens to the person you love feels as though it's happening to you.

I'm a Sephardic Jew and speak fifteenth century Spanish with my parents. When I was little and hurt myself, my mother would say, "Yo para ti," which means, "I for you." She was saying, "I wish I were in your place." I didn't understand then, but now that I have children of my own I do. If anything bad happens to my children, I wish I could take their place. It would hurt less.

This is very interesting, but what does friendship have to do with it?

In ancient Greek, the words *love* and *friend* had the same root word. This made me think. A friend is someone you love, someone you care for so deeply that whatever happens to that person also happens to you.

So, a friend is someone you love. Is that all?

A friend is someone you trust. You can turn your back to a friend. He won't stab you. If he does, who did he really stab? Himself! Because you belong to each other emotionally. Hurting one hurts the other. That is what friendship is all about. "One for all and all for one!" There is a symbiotic relationship between you. You benefit or lose together depending upon what each of you does.

But how does all this relate to management?

If you want to implement decisions efficiently, you must make sure that all the people you need to implement those decisions have common interests. There must be a win–win climate, a symbiotic relationship such as friends feel for each other.

But that is utopian. In the short run, at least, the reality is a conflict of interests. Even friends have conflicting interests from time to time.

Right. If you want a symbiotic, friendly, win–win climate, you must have mutual trust.

The way to transform potentially destructive conflict into constructive conflict is to create a nurturing symbiotic environment. Symbiotic means the parties perceive proposed change as eventually working for the benefit of all involved.

If there is mutual trust, you and I will perceive the mutual benefit of change and allow it to happen. Without mutual trust, there will be lots of resistance. The highest symbiotic relationship is love.

Can you define love for me? You have used this word too many times already and I am starting to wonder.....

For a two–party relationship to benefit from one another, one has to give, the other has to reciprocate. Where there is mutual trust, the time lag for the exchange can be longer than if there were no mutual trust. In a loving relationship there is no lag time between giving and getting paid back. The giving is the taking. The benefit of the taking is in the giving. When you take your kids to the circus, do you take them because you trust they will pay you back when you are old and feeble? Or do you do it for the pleasure of seeing them giggle, laugh, clap, and rejoice? Love is when the giving is the taking; love is when you don't keep an account of what you do for the person you love, when you give because the giving enriches you, the more you give the richer you are. The ones who truly possess this love are those who give it all: Buddha, Moses, Jesus Christ...

Mother Teresa?

Or the volunteer who helps people with AIDS or the volunteer for the homeless or a diligent worker or a responsible manager. They are all givers and the more they give the closer they get to their spiritual founders, who all share the biggest giver of them all—our God, the same God for us all whether we are Jews, Hindus or born–again Christians. We all have the potential to give. We are all made in God's image. By allowing ourselves to love and give. The ultimate trust is trusting the universe, God, the tao, a higher consciousness. Giving to others for the purpose of enriching ourselves happens when we love as a parent loves the children he or she takes to the circus. Without love we'll feel miserable sitting at the circus because of all the work we've left undone at the office. We'll get upset when we see these kids clapping their little hands about something we think is quite frivolous. Without love we need to take continuously, and the more we need to take the poorer we feel, and the poorer we perceive ourselves, the more miserable we feel because there is no end to the taking.

When a manager is given an organization to manage, he must create and nurture a win–win climate, a symbiotic environment based on mutual trust. Leaders, parents, and managers have a common purpose in creating this environment. This is the nurturing of the spiritual core of the organization by nurturing and giving out love for others as a way of life. Here's the way it would look on our master diagram.

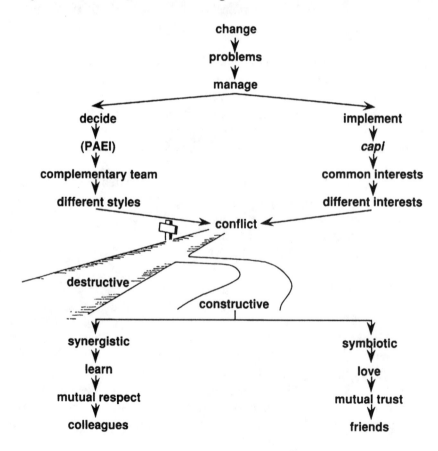

Now let's put it all together.

Conflict is a by-product of change. It can be destructive or constructive depending on whether mutual respect and trust exist. *Mutual respect is necessary so conflict can be constructive, so we can learn from each other's differences and make better decisions. Mutual trust* is necessary so we can perceive that a win-win climate will exist in the future. Then the people involved will cooperate in implementing decisions. When all of the above occurs, we have constructive, not destructive, conflict.

Which is more important, trust or respect?

Think about it. Can you trust people you don't respect?

Yes, I can. They may not be as intelligent as I would like them to be, but I also know they wouldn't knowingly hurt me.

Can you respect people you don't trust?

Only with great difficulty. If I don't trust the people, I probably won't listen to them either.

Exactly. Trust has to be established before respect can be established.

This is true for a society too, isn't it? There can be no democratic process in the Soviet Union if they do not stay together, not in spite of their differences, but because of them. They have to believe that in the long run, together is better than alone. Trust has to precede respect. Economic structural change, or perestroika, has to take place before full political freedom, or glasnost, is allowed.

Yes. If they don't change self-interests into common interests, political freedom may be used to express the different self-interests, and the USSR could disintegrate.

And it's true in a marriage as well. There is no respect unless there is trust first. That's why we usually say "trust and respect" rather than "respect and trust." Interestingly enough, I've noted that there is no happenstance in how people use words. Folk expressions are full of wisdom!

A Jewish rabbi once said, "Kabdehu ve hashdehu," which means, "respect and suspect." Respect all human beings, but watch out for their self interests. They are entitled to their opinions, but check their motives. What is legitimately good for them might not be good for you. Respectfully suspect.

Now that you have summarized it, I understand what we have discussed so far. But I wonder, exactly how do you manage an organization with mutual respect and trust. Most aren't managed that way, so your theory applies to only a handful of organizations in which trust and respect are an integral part of the culture.

I have not stopped with theory. I have worked out a process to change organizations so that they can produce the trust and respect they need. It doesn't happen just by talking about it. It takes commitment and hard work. And when you develop such an organization, it doesn't maintain that trust and respect for long unless you keep repeating the process that nurtures the desired culture. Every system tends toward entropy unless you put energy into it.

How do you create such an organization? How do you convert an organization with no mutual respect and trust to one that has both?

It requires changing the organizational structure and/or the process of decision making and/or the people's attitudes or the people themselves.

Why change the structure, for instance?

Environment determines behavior. An organization's structure determines, in part, an organization's behavior. The organization's structure determines the distribution of responsibility, authority and rewards. That distribution determines the differentiation of self–interests. Also, different tasks attract different kinds of people.

You need a structure that allows managers a place for their style in an environment where they can flourish. *(P)* tasks, for instance, attract people with a *(P)* style.

However, structure is not enough. Since people have different styles, they must learn how to communicate with each other. A correct process of participatory decision–making is necessary. We need to fix the structure and process of decision–making in order to create an environment of mutual trust and respect.

But sometimes, even changing the organizational environment isn't enough. Some people carry a chip on their shoulders and neither command nor grant respect or trust. They had a distrusting, disrespectful attitude before they joined the organization, so changing the environment will have no immediate effect on their style and attitude.

If you want to change an organization's behavior, you must treat its structure and decision–making process *and* the people themselves.

In what sequence?

Start with the process. Change how people decide. Then, using the new process, change the distribution of responsibility, authority, power, influence, and reward structures, which will enable you to deepen the process changes. This will enable you to further realign the structure.

As you repeatedly change the structure and processes, people's styles will change too. Their behavior will change. Those who can't change will probably leave the organization.

This sounds either too complicated or too simple.

It's neither. It's a process that doesn't exploit trust and respect. Instead, it develops a system that creates and nurtures respect and trust.

Too many consultants preach trust and respect but don't know how to create it. They raise hopes which, if not satisfied, make people skeptical of management theory and of consultants. It's not surprising that business schools have been accused of being irrelevant and that consulting is considered the second oldest profession.

I experimented over many years with organizational cultures that suffered from mistrust and disrespect and developed this methodology to change the culture to one that's governed by trust and respect. It required developing the right structure, process, and people.

People often make a key mistake when trying to change an organizational culture. They ignore structure and process and focus exclusively on people. If there is no teamwork, they fire the people and replace them with others who are thought to have respect and trust. But this doesn't necessarily work.

With the wrong structure and process, even well–meaning people start behaving in a destructive and disrespectful manner. The environment causes people to change their behavior, never mind how well–meaning they are.

This has been a rich but tiring conversation. Can we proceed tomorrow? I have enough food for thought to last me a while. You even made me want to go to my congregation and pray.

When you pray, you accept your vulnerability. You accept that you are part of a bigger system of consciousness, that your deeds matter because you belong and you affect the totality as that totality affects you. This prayer can be a reading, a chapter of the Bible, or a verse, but it doesn't have to be only the Bible or a prayer book.

Do not *(A)* your prayer; *(I)* it. You can do it by whistling, or meditating, or breathing, or practicing your love, whatever way you feel (I)ntegrated with the totality you belong to.

Conversation 10

Mutual Trust And Respect
And Quality of People

Could you please summarize what we've covered?

Okay, but let's do it together. In order to manage we need to decide and implement. It's impossible to make good decisions all alone all the time. We need to consult with others. We need a complementary team composed of different people with different points of view. Naturally, this generates conflict.

But we make it work by creating a climate of mutual respect, so we can learn from each other. We create a group of colleagues.

We always seek a complementary person. What I'm saying isn't anything new. The Old Testament says that the perfect spouse is *ezer keneged*. These Hebrew words mean "helpful against." Rabbis have debated the meaning of this phrase extensively. How can a spouse be helpful if he or she is against you? My explanation is that a spouse is helpful *because* he or she stands against the spouse's arguments; he or she can anticipate problems with a decision and thus enrich the solution and the relationship.

161

We look for someone who will complement our argument by pointing out the weaknesses. By incorporating criticism, the argument grows stronger.

That is, if there is mutual respect.

Absolutely. Conflict does not destroy a marriage. Conflict is to be expected because we each fell in love with and married someone who was different from us. What destroys a marriage is not what we fight about, but *how* we fight.

A study conducted at Yale University followed a select group of married couples over many years. The purpose was to find the personality traits that predict which couples will stay together. What they found is very interesting. There are no personality traits that predict who will stay married. Instead, they found that what predicts the survivability of marriages is not the differences in personalities, but *how* the couples handle the differences. I believe it is the mutual respect factor that determines how the differences are handled.

Marriage counselors are reporting something else very interesting. The reasons people divorce are the same reasons they marry.

We are attracted by our differences, not similarities. Since we know we are not perfect individually, we often choose a mate who is strong in areas where we are weak. This is wonderful before we get married, but what might happen later? The differences that were so attractive before become a source of difficulty later. People who cannot handle those differences end up divorcing or suffering a lot. The very same reason why two people got married is why they might wish to divorce: the differences attracted and then repelled them. Their styles are different. One is slow, the other fast; one is expressive, the other passive. Another source of conflict, especially in modern families, is conflicting interests brought about by dual careers. What is good for one might hurt the interests of the other. Couples should not dream about a utopian marriage in which there is going to be no conflict. Expect conflict and learn how to harness it, rather than run away from it or get depressed about it.

But conflict can be constructive.

Sure. For example, in some marriages, conflict is a source of binding. Sex is better after the fight. Couples are more intimate after their conflict than before. They grow closer. Other couples grow further apart from fight to fight. What is the difference? It is not the content of the conflict, but how they handle it.

You have probably had a fight with your spouse or someone else close to you. Years later, you don't remember the details of the fight, but you never forgot how it was fought. You still get a bad taste in your mouth remembering it. What you will never forget is whether you can trust and/or respect that person. It is mutual trust and respect that make conflict constructive or destructive. I have advice for you: anytime you disagree with someone, watch closely *how* you disagree more than *what* you disagree about.

> *I must respect people in spite of their being different in style and judgment.*

And develop a system that nurtures mutual trust in spite of the conflict of interests.

Management excellence can be achieved in an organization of colleagues who communicate well and who are also friends and thus who cooperate. They have mutual respect and trust for each other, so they have both synergistic and symbiotic relationships.

> *I can see the banner covering the building:*

Managerial excellence through teamwork: cooperation, communication, mutual trust and respect.

Not bad!

> *But how do we know whether we have that communication, cooperation, respect, and trust?*

You can see it in body language. When a decision is made in a climate of mutual respect, people turn to each other. They congregate and make decisions together. They face each other. Once they agree on a decision, if they also trust each other, they can afford to turn their back to each other when implementing the decision.

In a climate without mutual respect and trust, body language is just the opposite. Because people don't respect each other's opinions, they will most likely turn their backs to each other during decision making. When they set out to implement the decision, because they don't trust each other, they will face each other and watch each other.

Tell me which way you face during decision making and implementation, and I will tell you how well managed your organization is.

Is there another way to tell how well managed an organization is?

Yes. Making a decision together, rather than individually, takes more time. In organizations managed with mutual respect, it takes a long time to make a decision because people make it together. But implementation is swift. People trust each other to perform the assigned tasks. They don't try to play backseat driver with each other. In a badly managed organization, where there is no trust and respect, people make decisions very fast because they make them individually. But implementing takes forever, because of the backseat driving and continuous second guessing. Well managed organizations manage the "long–short" way, while badly managed organizations take the "short–long" way.

This helps me understand the Japanese approach to management as compared to the American. In the United States, decisions are made quickly but implementation is slow. In Japan, it takes a long time to make decisions, but implementation is fast.

The Japanese are successful and act quickly *because* they make decisions together slowly. A German manager once asked me, "How come the Japanese are so fast with innovations? We have the same R&D budget!" I said, "They are faster because they are slow." He thought I was trying to be funny.

The Japanese practice a lot of mutual respect. One characteristic of Japanese culture is that losing face is shameful. One may even be driven to commit hara–kiri because of it. And to make somebody else lose face is even worse.

What about mutual trust?

Japanese companies are committed to the employee for the long term and expect the same commitment in return. This mutual commitment creates a climate of mutual trust. And it is this trust which nourishes a win–win climate and encourages cooperation.

> *Unfortunately, it's not always that way in America. Sometimes management takes care of itself first and the employees later, if at all. When a company is in trouble, management uses its golden parachutes and fires the workers. Then Americans are surprised that unions don't necessarily want to cooperate with management. Why should they?*

If both sides could develop mutual trust and respect, it would be beneficial to both. When you trust, you care; and when you care, you listen; and when you listen, you learn. The end result is a symbiotic synergistic relationship.

Some relationships are only synergistic without being symbiotic. Democracy, capitalism, a market economy—these systems are designed for growth. They are synergistic but not symbiotic; the rich might get richer while the poor get poorer. Conversely, the socialist system tries to coalesce interests—the proletariat, intelligentsia, farmers—into a classless society. Socialists try to create a symbiotic society, but it certainly isn't synergistic. As British Prime Minister Winston Churchill observed, "Capitalism is an unequal distribution of wealth. Communism is an equal distribution of poverty."

> *So what do we need? Both systems?*

Yes. A true social democratic system that is both synergistic and symbiotic. In other words, one that prospers and grows while protecting the common interest of the total society.

The Common Denominator of Success
The success of any system—whether it is micro or macro, whether it is a single human being, a family, an organization, or a society—can be predicted by one and only one factor: the ratio between external and internal marketing.

$$\text{Success} = f \left\{ \frac{\text{external marketing}}{\text{internal marketing}} \right\}$$

External marketing is the amount of resources an organization invests in identifying and satisfying client needs. Internal marketing is how much managerial energy is needed to make something within the organization happen. External marketing is a function of market segmentation and product differentiation, among other things. Internal marketing is a function of mutual trust and respect. If there is little or no mutual respect or trust, the energy spent on internal marketing will be very high.

Since human energy, at any point, is fixed, the amount of energy available for external marketing depends on how much energy is spent on internal marketing. If all energy is spent internally, nothing is left for external marketing, since internal marketing takes precedence.

If people suffer from low self–esteem, low self–respect, and low self–trust, they'll be riddled with inner conflicts. They may be good looking, smart, and rich, yet they will be unable to have a successful relationship or career. Most of their psychological energy is spent dealing with problems that stem from their low self–respect and self–trust.

Could you elaborate on that?

When human beings lack self–respect and self–trust, most of their energy is spent on themselves. They are worried about what people think about them. They are trying to find out who they are and what they should do. Little is left over to deal with the outside. Before they can meet someone else and develop a relationship, they must first develop a relationship with themselves. They must learn to respect and trust themselves first.

The secret to finding the other person is finding yourself first. As a friend of mine, Jivan, once said, "If you don't spend so much time looking for the right person, you might become the one."

You probably know of some physically good–looking people who have little or no success with the opposite sex. At the same time, you probably know people who are not especially attractive but who are very much in demand. What is happening? The first type exudes no energy. Lacking self trust and respect, these people project indecisiveness and self rejection. The other type, who do respect and trust themselves, have all their energy available to focus on their partners. They are attractive because they exude energy. The condition for loving others is loving yourself first, but that does not mean being selfish. It means having mind, body, emotions, and spirit all in synchronicity and having trust and respect for those four aspects of one's self when they are in conflict.

Respecting your own vulnerability and weakness and trusting that you will eventually find the right solution is the secret of success. Success is not the destination, but the condition of your journey. Self–respect and self–trust means having faith in yourself—a precondition for having faith in others. There is no faith unless you love yourself, and to love yourself means to accept your inner conflicts and integrate your mind, body, emotions and spirit into a whole. It is this peacefulness and self–acceptance that makes people attractive or beautiful.

People who are in inner conflict are tense and spread pain around them. They are neither good spouses nor good managers. Having a face–lift, driving fancy cars, or indulging in other forms of conspicuous consumption will make them attractive, but only for a short while at best.

Educating our children means instilling trust and respect. Self–trust and self–respect. Respect for the body and for the emotions. Respect for parents, elders, teachers, the society we live in and, yes, respect for the flag. It is more important to educate children to "be" rather than to "know." What children know will often become obsolete in a very short time. Who they are will last a lifetime.

> *You know, I think the (A)s took over educational institutions. They measure know–how ad nauseam with standardized testing. It's an efficient education, but I doubt its effectiveness. It does not teach you to be. It teaches you to know.*

I agree, but let's continue and look at the next level of analysis. Let's assume that we have people who are "centered" and have self–respect and self–trust. They have energy to deal with the outside world, except that they have a disastrous family situation devoid of respect and trust. They have problems with their parents or spouses or children. Where is their energy spent now? Research shows that executives who go through a divorce are practically useless to the corporation for about three years. They can't succeed during that time, not because they are objectively bad, but because at that point in time subjectively their energy is going somewhere else. For them, success is to survive the upheaval with the fewest permanent scars possible. One source, and it might be a major one, for the very slow rise of productivity in the United States is the breakdown of the American family. One thing is certain: low American productivity is not caused by a lack of technology or financial resources.

Let's take the next level now: people who know who they are and who they are not and have a supportive, respectful and trusting family. All their energy is available to deal with their career, but their organizations have no mutual respect and/or trust. Co–workers walk with their backs against the wall for fear of being stabbed. Marketing is fighting sales; production is fighting engineering; accounting is fighting everyone. When the client arrives, what can a person say? "Come back tomorrow. I am exhausted today."

Now let's assume we have an organization with the right structure, process, and people. It has developed and nurtured mutual respect and trust, but it operates in a society riddled with corruption and hatred between religions, nationalities, and races. Now what? Can it compete well internationally? Where is the energy of that country going? How much energy is there left if the unions fight management, the military fights the government, and the government fights the people? Without respect and trust, where is the money going? To Switzerland! The country can be rich in gold and mines and land, but it cannot succeed because its relationships are bankrupt.

Compare the successful economies of Japan and Switzerland, nations with few physical resources, to some of the developing nations rich in oil, gas, diamonds and other resources. The developing nations can't use the resources constructively because of their tribalism and internal conflicts. Colonial powers exploited them, and the native governments often behave the same way after independence. The colonial powers brought to their colonies the missing elements of *(A)* and *(E)*. In order to dominate, the colonial powers, particularly England, would often dis(I)ntegrate a colony by turning one religious or ethnic group against the other. (The English excelled in this Roman strategy of divide and conquer. When the colonialists left, they took away the *(E)* and left behind a huge *(A)* and a broken *(I)*, thereby causing low *(P)*. This is the inheritance of many Third World countries.

Thus the tragedy of colonialism is not what the colonists took, but the culture and system they left behind or reinforced—a culture of elitism, exploitation, control, and bureaucracy. Third World countries now need to bring the weakened *(I)* component of their culture together. Peace first.

Peace among Muslims and Hindus. Peace in Angola and peace in South Africa. Only after *(I)* grows can these countries build group (E)ntrepreneurship through participatory management, as the Japanese now practice. As *(E)* increases, the next job will be to debureaucratize the government, i.e., reduce *(A)*. Then *(P)* will start growing.

> *Success, then, is a function of who you are, rather than what you have.*

Absolutely. What you have is the result of who you are, while who you are is not the result of what you have.

So, what do all the above examples illustrate? That SUCCESS COMES FROM WITHIN.

Too many companies worry exclusively about strategic planning and about how to beat their competitors. They are like the universe: expanding in the margins while collapsing at the core. Success comes from the inside. If we are strong inside, we can deal with any outside problem and handle it as an opportunity. If we are weak inside, then every outside opportunity will be perceived as a problem.

The Japanese success is not the core of America's problem. It is the manifestation. The problem with America is America, not Japan. It is the American system that has less mutual respect and trust than the Japanese. And who are the Americans beating? Societies with even less mutual respect and trust than the American system. True, we have to take into account other factors such as size and resources, but just imagine how much more these countries could be doing if they could capitalize on mutual respect and trust.

In a recent lecture in Johannesburg, I said that "South Africa is at the major intersection in its history. It can become the Switzerland or the Balkans of Africa. It will depend on whether it can develop a culture of mutual respect and trust."

> *So the way to improve a company's or a country's or a person's performance is not by changing strategy, but by changing the internal environment. Right?*

Right. Once you change the internal environment, the right strategy and direction will emerge more easily. Without it, even the best strategy will have great difficulty being implemented.

But if that's true, some countries could become empires.

Sure. Israel, for example. Israel has people from more than seventy different countries who have come together after being separated for two thousand years. It is a true United Nations. The differences create a tremendous amount of energy. If that energy were channeled with mutual respect and trust, Israel could become an empire.

What stands in its way?

Jewish people, for historical reasons, were prohibited from having a country of their own and from doing manual labor. They were therefore unable to develop strong *(P)* and *(A)* traits, and developed strong *(E)* and *(I)* qualities instead. For *(E)s*, respect is a challenge. *(E)s* are usually quite arrogant and feel they know better than others. Trust is another problem for *(E)s*. They have strong tendencies toward paranoia. Furthermore, for Jews, especially after thousands of years of persecution culminating in the Holocaust, trust does not come easily. Increasing the level of respect and trust in Israel would take more than just talking. And in light of the Jewish historical experience, realistically speaking, Israel can't take chances and act "as if" it trusts the world.

What other regions could become empires?

Europe, after 1992, could be a giant. It will be rich with cultural diversity, a market economy and open borders. It will become a serious contender for world leadership if it can overcome a history of disrespect and mistrust. If it does, the United States and Japan will have a serious competitor.

Can this model of yours predict which countries will succeed over time and which will not?

I think so. In the beginning, dominant countries like ancient Egypt were rich in resources such as gold, wheat, and people. Egyptians were strong in *(P)*; they produced or provided. Then *(A)* became the dominant factor as seen with the Roman Empire. The Ottoman empire was a combination of *(A)* and *(I)* because it was very tolerant of other religions and cultures. British colonialism was based on exporting *(A)*.

America advanced the age of *(E)*ntrepreneurship as a source of success. And other countries followed suit. That brings us to the present. The future, then, is for those nations who will be the strongest spiritually, in *(I)*. Right now, Japan leads the way.

That was very interesting. Looking at our chart, or map, I notice something that you haven't explained yet. Why is the road to destructive conflict a straight highway, while the path to constructive conflict appears to be a complicated route?

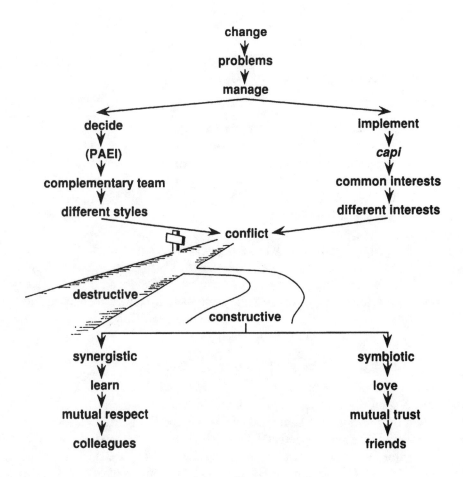

Because the road to destructive conflict *is* a straight highway. There is nothing you need to do to make conflict destructive. It is destructive by itself because of change. For example, if you leave a machine unused and unattended for a while, it won't start. "But I didn't do anything to it," you might complain. That's right, and that's why it won't work.

I know a man whose wife served him with divorce papers. He was surprised and crushed by the breakup of his marriage. "I didn't do anything," he said. A marriage is won or lost each day. Time is change, and unattended change is destructive by its own nature. This is the principle of entropy, in which every system naturally tends toward chaos unless energy is added. To make change constructive, you have to work on it.

But why the complicated path?

So that only people who drive slowly and carefully can see the sign pointing to the exit.

Why slowly? What's written on that sign?

"Mutual trust and respect." Have you ever noticed how people in conflict behave? They are in pain. And what do they do when they feel pain?

They "speed it up."

Yes! They speed straight down the highway of destructive conflict. They raise their voices, talk faster, call other people dirty names, or even storm out of the room. What's happening? They can't take the pain. Those that relax, slow down, and keep a cool head have a chance to resolve the conflict or at least understand it so they can handle it. They're the ones who can see the sign and take the constructive road.

And how do you slow down?

The tougher the situation is, the more relaxed everyone needs to be. I have found by working with senior executives around the world that the most successful ones are those I call "duck managers." If you look at a duck, it floats along on top of the water, appearing calm, but under the water its feet are paddling as fast as they can. Likewise, a good manager can be relaxed in spite of the conflict. He doesn't lose his head or his objectivity about a subject. He never expresses conflict in a destructive, disrespectful way.

You mean a good manager is a person who knows how to disagree without being disagreeable?

That's right. "Think Yiddish, act British". Or to quote an English proverb which comes from a Latin proverb: "Use soft words and hard arguments." And it applies not only to managers, but to spouses, children, parents, everyone. Some people do the opposite and agree disagreeably. Even if you reach an agreement with them, you don't want to repeat the experience. It was too painful.

Yes, I know. Arguing with emotional people is exhausting.

This is true in international relations too. How we handle our enemy is extremely important. Never show disrespect to your enemy. You will never find peace that way. Even wars have to be handled respectfully. You must communicate trustworthiness or the end of one war will simply sow the seeds for the next one.

There is a report that then Secretary of State Henry Kissinger prevented the Israelis from advancing too far into Egypt during the Yom Kippur War in 1973. Egypt must not be crushed, Kissinger claimed, or Israel would never find peace. As in the East, you must always leave a way for your opponent not to lose face, or the next time you will face a far more determined enemy. A way out means your opponent should not lose respect and trust. Otherwise they will have to fight again to regain it.

After World War II, the United States wisely proposed the Marshall Plan to Europe, including Germany. The United States reconstructed Germany. If it had not done so, Germany would not be part of NATO today, and it would have harbored the same resentments it did after World War I, which sowed the seeds for World War II.

A system must be based on trust and respect and should control any attempts to destroy that base. The Israeli Supreme Court justifiably barred the late Rabbi Meir Kahane's political party, claiming its militantly anti–Arab platform was racist. Democratic societies act properly when they ban parties that are anti–democratic and have no respect for the democratic process. Otherwise, totalitarian political parties are allowed to gain power democratically and then avoid and abolish the democratic system that allowed them to gain that power, as the Nazi party did. This should not be allowed. The philosopher Herbert Marcuse expressed this well when he wrote, "There can be no tolerance toward systems that renounce tolerance."

The political application of mutual trust and respect make me think differently, but right now I need to concentrate on management. Tell me more about the kinds of people needed to make conflict constructive.

To make conflict constructive, one of the factors we must focus on is the people; we must have people who command, and grant, respect and trust. Now, the question is: What kind of people command, and grant, respect and trust?

For staff people (as opposed to line managers, who have to direct people), what they know is more important than who they are. Say they have a functional responsibility in marketing, data processing, or accounting. You may be able to put up with their individual style as long as they know their professional field. But once people become line managers, who they are is more important than what they know. If they don't know something, they can hire whomever they need and get staff people to advise them. A very successful corporate president once told me, "I have three doctorates although I never finished high school." I asked him how he did that. "Easy. I hired them." Know–how is easy to get; you can just hire good people. To "be" is much more difficult.

But what do you do with people who do not grant respect and trust?

Recommend them to your competitors. That will undermine those companies more than your competitive products. Sow dissension within your competition and emerge victorious while you surround yourself with people who command, and grant, respect and trust.

What about people who have only one of these characteristics? For instance, what if they command respect but don't give it?

That's not good in the long run, and with people who give respect but don't command it, that's not good even in the short run. If the people aren't trustworthy, I don't care how much they know, they cannot succeed as managers, leaders, or parents. Period.

Tell me how much respect you command and grant, how trusting and trustworthy you are, and I'll tell you whether you're a good manager or not. For that matter, I'll tell you whether or not you are a good leader of society or a good parent or a good spouse. In short, I'll tell you what kind of a human being you are.

So being the right kind of human being is part of managing well?

That is the essence of it all. A good manager (or parent, or spouse, or political leader) is not valued for what he knows but for who he is. It is easier to hire someone who "is" and teach him to know, than to hire someone who knows and teach him to be.

If we were to randomly read some résumés, we would find that what people write about themselves is (P) and (A) oriented. It's what they have done, what degrees they've earned and what titles they've held. It doesn't tell us much about who they are as human beings. Are they respected? Do they disagree in a way that is enriching to others? Do they even know how to disagree? The résumé does not say whether they are trustworthy. Maybe they're sharks who attack the moment they smell blood. Maybe they'll knife you if you turn your back on them. This information doesn't appear in a résumé, but in my judgment it's the most important thing managers need to know before hiring people.

How then do you decide whom to hire?

Call former employers to find out whether your applicants are trustworthy and respected. Ask how they contributed and how they handled disagreements. You want to know what kind of people they are.

Isn't it difficult to get that kind of information?

Yes. In the United States there are laws that make this information difficult to obtain.

So what should you look for?

Look for people who can command and grant respect. The first characteristic of such people is that their style is well rounded. That means they have no blanks in their code. *(P---)s*, for instance, are not good managers; they are mismanagers. But big *(P)s* with small *(aei)s* are normal managers. They are (P)roducers. They'll be good first line supervisors but won't go beyond that unless they are flexible and willing to learn and change.

It's important not to have any blanks in the code. In a complementary team, people have to link up. People with blanks in their code cannot link up with people who excel in that missing role. Also, people who are not well rounded will have considerable difficulty changing and growing.

You need individuals who are aware of their strengths and weaknesses. When you interview someone for a job, one of the first questions should be, "What are your strengths and what are your weaknesses?" The person who says, "I don't have any weaknesses," or "My weaknesses are my strengths," shouldn't be hired. People who don't know their weaknesses don't know who they are. I would be afraid of working with them or for them.

Why would they be a problem?

To command and grant respect, you have to know who you are. Only by knowing who you are will you be able to identify what other styles you need to build a complementary team.

I can identify the management styles of those around me, yet I'm having difficulty identifying my own style in (PAEI) terms.

This is common. My friend, Professor Sam Culbert of the John E. Anderson Graduate School of Management at UCLA, says, "It takes two to know one." None of us knows himself in a vacuum. We see ourselves through the eyes of others. We know ourselves through the impact we have on others. Logically, if we know the managerial style of others, it makes sense that others will know our own style. They respond to or cope with our style. That's why Lone Rangers develop go–fers and Bureaucrats have yes–yes clerks. And Arsonists cause people to become claques.

So if you want to know who you are, watch the impact you have on others. Be sensitive to how people react to you. Watch how your subordinates and peers behave.

That reminds me of an experience I had. Many years ago, I was lecturing in Mexico. I spoke English and was assisted by a simultaneous translator. I grew tired of the translation because the audience was reacting to the material a minute later. My lecture was out of sync, so I asked the audience if it would prefer if I spoke in fifteenth century Spanish: a mixture of Italian, Portuguese, and Spanish. As I mentioned before, I spoke fifteenth century Spanish with my family. The audience agreed.

It was quite arrogant on my part to lecture twentieth century material in an archaic language, but I tried and something very interesting happened. The audience reacted to a certain word as if they did not understand me. I had asked them in fifteenth century Spanish, "Did you hear me?" They winced as if I had said something very strange, so I asked in English, "What did I say?" Someone answered, "Well, you asked us if we *felt* you."

I said, "No! I asked, 'Did you *hear* me?'"

And someone said, "Oh no! The verb "to hear" in modern Spanish is *escuchar* and you were using the word *sentir*, which means 'to feel.'"

At that moment, I had an illumination. Five hundred years ago, the senses of hearing, feeling, and listening could all be expressed in one word: *sentir*. It really means "to sense." Even today, in modern Spanish, when somebody is hard of hearing, people say he or she is *mal de sentido*, which literally means "hard of feeling."

What has happened over the last five hundred years? In Spanish, we now have several words instead of one to describe the same thing. It means we can separate the phenomena.

It means some people can hear without listening, and some people listen but don't feel what you say. They can repeat every word, even analyze them, but they don't *feel* what you say. Five hundred years ago, since "hear" was only one word, it meant that people heard, listened and felt what they heard. They were more in touch with each other.

I had another illumination when I was in Chicago one cold winter. I was driving my car in a big snow storm. Outside it was freezing, but inside the car it was so warm that I removed my jacket. I sat only one and a half inches away from the freezing cold, yet I was very comfortable. The same phenomenon occurs emotionally in modern life.

Technology has trained us to tune out. We box ourselves in. Out there, people are falling apart emotionally, but we keep within our own space and pay no attention to them. We have learned how to separate *feeling* from *hearing* from *listening*. Consider the expression "tune out." We treat people like a radio station we don't want to listen to.

For some people, the time it takes to make the transition from hearing to listening to feeling is quite long. My dog senses instantly how I feel when I get home from work. As soon as I walk through the door, he either jumps on me or, if I am upset, goes to his corner, curls into a ball, and waits. On the other hand, it takes me forever to communicate how I feel to a person I know. By the time that person hears, then listens, then feels, I am even more upset.

Let's summarize. For good management we need mutual trust and respect, which means that good managers are people who command, and grant, respect. What sort of people are they? First, their style is well rounded. They don't excel in everything, but they're capable of adequately performing all roles. They have strengths and weaknesses, but no blanks in their *(PAEI)* code.

Second, good managers know themselves. A way to know yourself is by paying attention to what you do to others. Are you aware of how others respond to you? That will tell you who you are. Good managers are people who hear, listen, and feel. They do not just hear without listening or listen without feeling. They are sensitive to the impact they have on others. They are conscious. They are present.

People who don't know themselves are usually the ones who think they know exactly who they are. They live in a vacuum; they don't allow feedback from the outside.

Good managers accept their strengths and their weaknesses, because the first condition for accepting the weaknesses of others is accepting your own. If you cannot accept yourself, how will you accept others?

> *I hear you loud and clear. Mutual trust and respect must begin with self-respect and self-trust. These qualities grow from the inside out. To achieve good management, first look inward. Anything else?*

Good managers can identify the strengths in other people that they lack in themselves. This is very difficult though. Big *(E)s* can identify other big *(E)s*, but they don't know how to identify and evaluate an *(A)*'s strengths. They don't know what criteria to apply. As a matter of fact, they don't even like *(A)s*.

That's why good managers have a well-rounded style. They are in touch with what they do, have a balanced view of themselves, accept their weaknesses, and can identify the strengths of others in areas where they are weak. Furthermore, they accept others who are better than they are in certain respects, because they accept that they are not good at everything. They can deal with the conflicts that stem from those differences. They are secure enough not to be threatened by disagreements. They can hear, listen, and feel. In essence, they can create a learning environment.

You're talking about people who are well balanced and self–actualized. Can you list all the qualities?

Sure. Good managers are people who:

1. have a well–rounded, flexible style
2. know themselves
3. are aware of their effect on others
4. have a balanced view of themselves
5. accept their own weaknesses
6. can identify strengths in others
7. accept others who are different
8. can harness conflict
9. create a learning environment

In short, they are mature people.

Yes, maturity makes good managers. Maturity comes from experience, and experience comes from making bad judgments and learning from them. The process of maturation is accompanied by pain. It involves losing attachments to your past to make space for new attachments in the future. Not everybody knows how to lose those attachments, how to let go. Winning is easy, losing is difficult. Show me a manager who comes out a winner after he loses, and I'll show you a good manager. The road to heaven is through hell.

So you are against the fast track which allows young business school graduates to start at the top of the management pyramid?

Absolutely. They are frequently propelled to the top by what they know, not by who they are. They don't have the experience that teaches them maturity and humility. Good managers know their weaknesses and seek the assistance of others. They have learned to be humble.

What matters in good managers or spouses or leaders is not what they know, but who they are. In Spanish there are three levels of knowing: (1) you can know *information*; (2) you can know *how to do* something; and (3) you can know *how to be*. Team leaders, especially managers, must know how to *be* if they want to command and grant respect and trust. In modern society we overemphasize the knowing of information, the "how to"s, and almost ignore the critical importance of the "how to be". One really wonders whether so–called developed nations, while developed economically, are really underdeveloped spiritually, and whether development on one level is not a repression on another level. As the so–called underdeveloped nations that are strong spiritually try to catch up economically their economic advancement may eventually result in a spiritual regression. They might sacrifice the "to be" to gain the "to know", and I am not sure it is a true gain. Thus one of the challenges for developing countries is how to develop economically without losing their traditionally strong family unity.

Are you agreeing with those countries that oppose importing American culture as depicted in movies and on tv? Do you agree with Iran that America is the devil? What are you saying?

I don't agree with the devil accusation, obviously. And I don't think you can stop the flow of one culture into another. The world, as Marshall McLuhan predicted, is not *becoming*, it already *is* a global village. But we should beware. The USA has done much good for the world with its example of freedom, democracy, and entrepreneurial systems. At the same time its materialism, if emulated with abandon, can be dangerous to a spiritual orientation.

May we have an intermission? I need time to think about all of this.

Okay. See you soon.

Conversation 11

Miscommunication

We discussed the people component—why we need mature people as team members—in our last conversation. We have not yet discussed the process factor.

Let's start from the beginning. To manage anything well, we have to make good decisions and then implement them using as little internal marketing energy as possible. When we're not managing well, we are either making bad decisions or implementing them in a more prolonged, painful, or expensive way than necessary.

We also said that in order to make good decisions we need a complementary team. Each member of the team should be a colleague whose differences of opinion team members respect and learn from. His or her style should complement the others by balancing their naturally biased judgments.

So for good decision making, we need a complementary team in which the members have different styles. That creates conflict and possibly miscommunication, even if each member of the team is mature and capable of handling conflict.

We have already covered some reasons why people miscommunicate. Let me summarize them, then we'll proceed to others. Later on we will discuss how to handle miscommunication that stems from the differences in style.

We determined that one difference is people's styles when they agree or disagree. If (E)ntrepreneurs disagree with an idea, they will usually be very expressive about it. They're expressive even when they agree.

Is that why we don't know whether they're agreeing or disagreeing half the time? They speak so animatedly, that it seems as if they're disagreeing.

Which can upset us. We might even feel we have to disagree with them, now that they have raised their voice to us. It seems they want to argue just for the sake of arguing.

That's why, when (E)s get together, it may appear they are disagreeing with each other, when actually they are reinforcing each other's arguments. What about (A)s?

When *(A)s* disagree, they are very calm. They just look at you, lower their chin, and freeze. That can cause miscommunication because *(E)s* interpret the silence as agreement when *(A)s* are actually disagreeing.

Also, we covered what the words "yes" and "no" mean, depending on who is speaking. For (E)ntrepreneurs, "yes" means maybe. When they say "no", they're definite, which is just the opposite with *(A)s*. When (A)dministrators say "no", it only means maybe; you can still come back and try to convince them. When they say "yes", they're determined.

I saw this happen when I was working with a CEO in Australia. He was one of the biggest *(E)s* I've ever worked with. When talking to his vice president of manufacturing, he asked, "Why don't we have a manufacturing facility in Brisbane? I mean, what's going on, guys?" His vice president asked, "Well, should we have one?"

The CEO said, "Yeah, why don't we?" So the vice president of manufacturing, who had a *(PAei)* style as we would expect, started planning to build the facility. Two months later, the CEO was very upset. "Why in hell are we building a factory in Brisbane?"

"You said we needed it," the vice president said.

"Can't I think out loud? I was just asking you why we don't have one. I didn't tell you to start building one!"

People often don't know whether (E)ntrepreneurs are thinking out loud or deciding. Sometimes when subordinates believe the *(E)s* are deciding, they discover it wasn't a decision and get blamed for acting on thoughts. The next time the *(E)* thinks out loud, the employees remember the last episode and don't act. The *(E)* then become upset because his staff didn't do what was expected of them.

The employees feel there is no way they can win. No matter what they do, they're going to be humiliated for something. (E)ntrepreneurs always act disappointed and disillusioned.

Now let me ask you, when does "yes" really mean yes, and "no" really mean no?

> *When (P)s say it. They don't understand what's going on when people question their yes or no. To them it's very simple and obvious. "Why can't people just communicate?" they ask.*

For which type is a "yes" a maybe, and "no" a maybe?

> *The (I)ntegrators. They are political animals.*

Right. In order to understand what "yes" and "no" mean, you can't define them according to your own dictionary. You have to look at *who* is saying them. You shouldn't listen with your own bias.

> *Explain what you mean by "listen with your own bias."*

In all the world's major religions—Buddhism, Judaism, Christianity, Islam—there is something called the Golden Rule. Do you know what that is?

> *Yes. "Don't do to others what you would hate to be done to you."*

And the corollary would be...

> *"Do to others what you would want done to you."*

Now these rules are the wrong approach to management communication. If you communicate with others as you want them to communicate with you, what mistake will you make? If you are an (E)ntrepreneur, you'll communicate to others as if they are...?

(E)s.

And that's wrong. You really have to focus on who you are talking to. I'm not saying anything new. If you go to the bank to apply for a loan, you're not going to wear loud or shabby clothing, are you? You'll probably dress conservatively, sit quietly, and answer the banker's questions politely. You are attempting to be responsive to his or her style. You are trying to act like a banker. That is exactly the point. Before you talk to people, you have to ask yourself, "*Who* am I talking to?" When people talk to you, you have to ask yourself, "*Who* is talking to me?" Then you can correctly interpret what they are saying and talk in a way they understand.

Why are you telling me this? It is interesting, but how does it relate to management?

Because one aspect of management is the selling of ideas. If you can't communicate and convince, you cannot manage. All sales people will tell you that you must know your clients. You have to focus on communicating to your clients so they will understand you even though each of them speaks what sounds like a different language.

Let's try to systematize this with a diagram that describes decision–making styles as they impact communication.

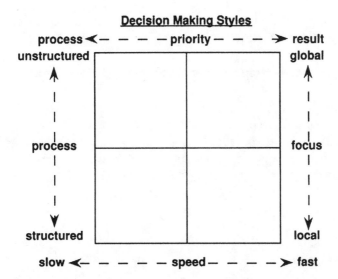

In the upper part, you have priorities. On the right side is result–orienta-tion, or the *what* and *why*. On the left side is process–orientation, or the *how* and *who*. Some people are results–oriented, while others pay more attention to the process. On the horizontal line at the bottom of the win-dow is the speed at which people make decisions. On the left side the decision making is slow, and on the right side it is fast.

What does all this mean?

It means that some people make decisions slowly. There's a joke about bureaucrats: you shouldn't tell bureaucrats a joke on Friday because they might laugh in church on Sunday. This is not true for (E)ntrepreneurs, who react very quickly. They will interrupt your joke because it reminded them of another joke.

What do the vertical lines stand for?

On the right side we have focus: global at the top; local at the bottom. This dimension corresponds to the window analogy we talked about before. One person may see the view while somebody else sees only the dirty frame. Some people have a global view, while others pay attention only to the details.

The last variable is the process by which people make decisions. Some processes are unstructured, others are structured.

What do those terms mean in this case?

In an unstructured process, a person may start talking about *A*, which reminds him of Z. Then he goes to Q, then to B, then to C, and finally, to X. He goes back and forth, because he is thinking in a holistic way; everything is related to everything else. In structured processes, however, people are linear. They don't like to start talking about B until they fully understand *A*. Then they don't want to start C until B is fully understood.

So?

If we look at the chart, we'll see that the four styles—(P)roducer, (A)dministrator, (E)ntrepreneur, and (I)ntegrator—will fit into the four boxes of this window. Who has the global, fast–moving, unstructured style of decision making?

The (E)ntrepreneurial types. I can see that.

Who is fast, structured, and focused on details and results?

The (P)s.

They are our railroad engineers. They are the ones who say, "Show me the tracks and get out of the way." In the workplace, they are the ones most likely to say, "What do we need to do? Let's go and do it. We have a business to run. Talk less, do more."

That makes sense.

Who has the structured, slow–moving style focused on process and details?

The (A)dministrators.

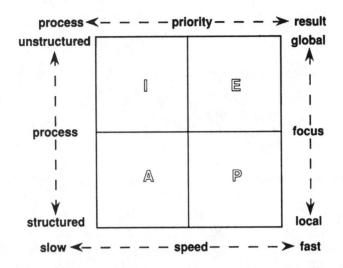

Now read the *(I)* style from the chart.

> *They are process–oriented, slow, and unstructured; and that is why*
> *they can be so politically astute. They have a global view. They can*
> *change and adapt.*

If we look at this diagram and the different styles of different people, we can see why they all may possibly miscommunicate.

The (E)ntrepreneurial types will be in conflict mostly with the types diagonal to them, the (A)dministrators. Mixing these two together is like mixing oil and water. It is going to be very difficult.

Can you give me some examples of these differences?

The (E)ntrepreneurs are very fast. They usually start thinking on their own. When an *(E)* goes to a meeting with an (A)dministrator, he has already started thinking in the corridor. By the time he hits the (A)dministrator's office, he's already moving at 150 miles an hour. He hits the *(A)* like a ton of bricks.

(A)s are slow, not because they are stupid, but because they are *thinking* about what the *(E)s* are saying, about the repercussions of their ideas. It takes them time to process each idea. When they get hit by the ideas of the (E)ntrepreneurs, it's like an avalanche. And they really have

difficulty handling it. For any single *(E)* idea there are at least ten repercussions that matter to *(A)s*. The (A)dministrators can't handle the load or the speed. Soon (A)dministrators stop thinking and listening. They just let ideas pass them by, accusing the *(E)s* of being full of hot air. The *(A)s* might start hoping the *(E)s* leave soon so they can get back to work.

And the silence of (A)dministrators is misconstrued by (E)s as agreement. Hmm.

There's more. *(E)s* don't like to make appointments. The moment they have an idea, they want to deal with it. They might show up unannounced at the *(A)s'* office, and (A)dministrators hate surprises. The *(A)s* have everything organized: their desk, their files, their day, their vacation, their year, their life—and here comes an unguided missile.

And (E)ntrepreneurs rarely have the patience to talk about the *how* dimension, the boring problems of implementation. They spend most of their time talking about *why* they are going to do something. *(E)s* are like eagles who see the whole countryside from above, and not necessarily any of the details.

The American Indians had totemic symbols for people.[9] When a warrior was called Big Eagle, this was a way of describing what we are calling an *(E)* style. He soared through the sky with a spectacular view of the horizon, but his feet were not on the ground. He lacked a full sense of reality.

The American Indians would have called the *(A)* style a buffalo—very slow and heavy, but once it decides to charge, watch out! The buffalo doesn't change direction easily. It would probably run you over first. Now, just imagine an eagle and a buffalo trying to charge together. It would be very difficult, wouldn't it?

What happens when (A)s try to talk to (E)s?

(A)s call ahead and schedule appointments which *(E)s* usually change or miss. When they finally meet, *(A)s* discuss so many details that it deeply annoys the *(E)s*. If you ask (A)dministrators about a problem, they usually start by explaining the past. They tell you how the problem evolved, as if you wouldn't understand the problem without knowing its history. *(A)s* always seem to start with Adam and Eve. After two hours, they're only up to the Renaissance. You have to meet for another four hours before finally

hearing about the present. *(E)s* and *(P)s* on the other hand, have the attention span of a squirrel.

Finally the *(E)s* will say, "Okay, enough history. What's the solution?" The *(A)s*, with a two–thousand–year view of the problem, will claim that it will take how long to solve it?

Another two thousand years.!

It's called paralysis from overanalysis. Bureaucrats suffer from it. They most often say, "Extremely difficult! It cannot be done."

Now the *(E)s* have a totally different time frame. They don't like looking at the past. For (E)ntrepreneurs, the past is dead. They are looking to the future. They're eagles flying high in the sky, looking beyond the horizon. They see opportunities, and they have difficulty communicating what they see because it is not yet clear. They sense it. If you ask them to describe it in detail, they will still describe it in generalities. Furthermore, *(E)s* dislike talking about problems. Their answer to a problem is, "It's *your* responsibility." For *(E)s* each problem is an opportunity to get excited about; for an *(A)* those opportunities are problems to worry about.

Aren't (E)s concerned with why problems exist?

No. They prefer to focus on opportunities. Problems drain them of energy.

What about the solution?

When you ask *(E)s* for a solution, they usually get upset.

Why?

Because they feel the opportunities they foresee should have been dealt with already. That's why it's usually uncomfortable working with *(E)s*; they get upset easily. What they don't realize is that they're flying at high altitude. Those buffaloes or those little rodents—*(P)s* would be called rodents in American Indian symbolism—are so close to the ground they can't see beyond their whiskers. They don't understand what the *(E)s* are talking about. They don't share the same vision.

What happens then when (A)s and (E)s get together?

The *(E)s* will usually run out of the room in the middle of the discussion. They just can't stand all the details. Then the *(A)s* feel ignored, abused, and abandoned. They feel they have no one who will listen to their problems. The *(A)s* feel they are working for sea gulls. If you have ever sailed, you know that sea gulls can be terribly bothersome. They appear from above, let out a shriek, drop a shot on your boat, and disappear only to reappear later on.

> *What about the other extreme, the case of (P)s communicating with (I)s?*

Task–oriented, fast–moving *(P)s* are usually not very personal or sensitive. This upsets the (I)ntegrators, who want to slow down and pay attention to people. They will usually accuse the (P)erforming types of being hatchet men, insensitive and "macho."

The *(P)s*, on the other hand, think *(I)s* are too feminine, too weak, and too slow. This is not an issue of sex, but of style. A woman can be a *(P)* and a man can be an *(I)*. As a matter of fact, I have observed a real flip–flop from the traditional sexual stereotypes in the United States over the last twenty years.

> *It doesn't sound as though these two get along any better than the (A)s and the (E)s.*

They don't. And they don't necessarily like each other, either, because each thinks the other is insensitive. *(P)s* think *(I)s* are insensitive to what the organization needs, while *(I)s* feel the *(P)s* are insensitive to how people feel. That can create hard feelings and a lack of mutual respect between the two types.

> *I understand the nature of these conflicts, but what do we do about them?*

Next time we meet, let's talk about how to handle the different styles. I call this bottom–up leadership. Many books have been written about how to lead employees. Let me talk about how to lead your boss, or how to sell your ideas to people who are different from you.

> *Good idea. Right now I need to get something to eat.*

How to Communicate with Others Whose Style is Different

Let's talk now about how to talk to people who are different from us. First, you understand we are not talking about communicating only with a boss. This pertains to communicating with peers as well. If you're dealing with your employees, the methodology is more difficult to use because we usually ignore an employee's style. That is a mistake. We need staff cooperation no less than we need the boss's cooperation. We should be even more conscious of how we deal with subordinates because we usually take lightly those we believe we can control. That's a mistake some people make with their spouse or children. They treat them with less respect than people they do not even know.

Start thinking about how to communicate with people in general. Think of people as if each one were your boss. This means you will have to sell your ideas without using authority or power, just your influence.

How do I do that? You say I should try to talk to people in their own language, but first I have to know who they are. Do you have any psychological tests that I can use to find out whether people are (P)s, (A)s, (E)s, or (I)s before I talk to them?

That would be futile. You can't refuse to talk to people unless they submit to psychological tests. As I have already told you, I don't recommend such tests even though certain ones can measure *(PAEI)*.

> *But if you don't know certain people very well or have never met them before, what do you do?*

Ask them what job they perform. Look at the organizational chart. If people are in marketing, expect them to be (E)ntrepreneurial. If they are in sales, they may be more of the (P)roducer type. If they're in accounting, they may have an (A)dministrative orientation. Look at their jobs; try to assess their behavior. Then verify your assessment.

> *How?*

Look at their offices. Look at their desk, clothes, posture, and energy. Be sensitive to them. It's not as important to quantify personality traits as it is to be conscious of whether they understand you or not. Then adapt your style so that you can communicate clearly.

And watch for this phenomenon. If two *(E)*s get together, the one who is a stronger *(E)* by nature might take on the *(P)* style as well, while the other *(E)* might assume the *(A)* and *(I)* styles. Remember, to make a good decision, all the *(PAEI)* roles must be performed.

> *When a "natural" (A) joins the discussion, the lesser (E) will at that point assume the (P) role, right?*

Right. And the *(A)* type will exhibit *(I)* tendencies. The environment, the nature of the task, and the other people involved have a large impact on what style a person exhibits. Natural inclinations are only a starting point. So don't be so fast to brand people. Observe them. Listen and feel. Use the tools from these conversations plus your own intuition.

> *This is complicated.*

Right. But life is not simple. All we are trying to do in these conversations is simplify life so that we can deal with its complexities.

> *Okay. What would you do when talking to (P)s, for example?*

(P)s are quick decision makers. They behave as if they don't have a lot of time. They're usually under pressure to deal with a crisis, so they must focus on results. Let me ask you a question. What if your boss were a (P), and you said to him or her, "I need you for three hours to discuss a problem." What would he or she say?

"Three hours? Sure, how about in ten years? Maybe by then I'll be able to find my desk!"

How much time can you request realistically?

Five or ten minutes, maybe fifteen at the very most.

Then try to be short. Start with the end of your argument, the purpose of your meeting. Give your boss the bottom line, because that's all he or she has time for. You can supply the support materials later. Start at the conclusion and answer questions later.

What do you do if the person is an extreme Lone Ranger, not just a (P)roducer?

Tell him or her it's a crisis. For the Lone Ranger, that's a legitimate reason to give you time. You should say, "We have a crisis and there is time pressure. We must deal with it immediately, and because of that I'm already applying the solution. I just need your approval."

Why would that work?

If you don't say you're under time pressure or that you're in the middle of implementing a solution, the Lone Ranger will say...

"Put it on my desk."

Then the problem will sit there with a hundred other problems, while you're stuck with no solution.

So, what should I do?

You really have to take the initiative with Lone Rangers. Since they're not going to delegate to you, you have to take initiative yourself. You have to legitimate what you do. You should say, "We have a crisis. I need five minutes of your time. Here is the problem, and here is what I am *already* doing. I just need your approval so I can finish the task." It's done! There you go.

Remember, with Lone Rangers the problem must be a crisis, there must be time pressure, and you must take initiative to solve it, or it will not be dealt with in a reasonable amount of time.

Now, will the same approach work with (A)dministrators? If you call an *(A)* and say, "We have a crisis and I'm already implementing the solution; I just need your blessing," what do you think would happen?

You'd be fired .

An *(A)* would say, "Who gave you the right to start implementing a solution? How dare you proceed with implementation without getting approval." The *(A)* will be precisely wrong. He or she runs a well–controlled disaster. Don't you dare take initiative until you get the *(A)'s* approval, even if the company is sinking.

If you are a *(P)* working for a Bureaucrat, you've probably made this mistake. You've probably had a crisis and solved it. When you went to your boss to get his or her blessing, you expected praise. You got quite a surprise instead. The fact is, you applied a *(P)'s* solution for an *(A)*, and the *(A)* didn't appreciate it at all.

What is the correct procedure with (A)s?

Bureaucrats or (A)dministrators, depending on how extreme their style is, are more interested in the *how* than in the *what*. Their style is slow and structured, with a focus on process. You have to fit your style to their style. They prefer form to function. So you must pay close attention to form. The first thing you must do is schedule an appointment. *(A)s* don't appreciate surprises. If you do pop up unexpectedly, they won't listen to you for the first half hour. They're upset because you caught them unprepared or because you came unprepared. Tell them in advance what the meeting is about so that they can get ready for you.

Next, you have to use what I call a "coefficient of error."

What's that?

(E)s and *(P)s* move quickly; *(A)s* and *(I)s* move slowly. They have different concepts of time. My style is *(E)*, and I have found that my coefficient of error is six. This means that if I tell my staff, "You can do this in one hour," it will really take six hours. If I tell them, "We can do that in a week," how long will it actually take?

Six weeks.

You see, for me as an eagle flying in the sky, one beat of my wings takes me a long distance with relative ease. However, those down on the ground have to run up and down canyons and hills to travel the same distance. Following my small movements from below is extremely difficult. But being an eagle up in the air, I might ignore the difference, which would cause an error in my expectations.

So before an *(E)* calls an *(A)* and says, "I need to meet with you for half an hour," the *(E)* should think about his coefficient. If it's a six like mine, the *(E)* should say, "I need a half hour meeting with you, but knowing me we had better schedule three hours."

What the *(A)* doesn't want is for you to schedule a half hour and then wind up staying three hours. The *(E)* must ask for three hours and tell the *(A)* what the agenda will be. No surprises.

Anything else?

Next, if you are an *(E)* or *(P)* talking to an *(A)* or *(I)*, I suggest you learn to slow down.

Slow down?

(E)s constantly run out of breath. Their mind moves faster than their lips. In Mexico they say, "The first one who stops talking to take a breath loses the argument."

I have noticed that in countries with an (E) culture it seems as though everyone talks at the same time. How do you suggest learning to slow down?

Let's say you are an *(E)* or a *(P)* dealing with an *(A)*. You arranged for a three hour meeting and told the *(A)* what you'd be discussing. Start by slowing down as you walk to the meeting. Take a deep breath and slow down. When you arrive, you should have slowed down to the *(A)'s* speed. For every one of your ideas, the *(A)* will think of many many repercussions. The *(A)* needs time to process your information. If you don't slow down in the corridor, do it during the first few minutes of the session. In modern society, it is not only the *(E)* style that causes the rushing. It is the *(P)* pressures to perform that cause people to run around breathless. Slow down! Start a meeting with a relaxation–response. Close your eyes and breathe deeply. Relax for a few seconds. This idea comes from **Dr. Ray Benson** of the Harvard Medical School.[10]

> *I know his work. But he recommends the relaxation–response to avoid the undesirable effects of stress.*

And stress and good decision making don't get along. The more relaxed you are the better your decision will be because you'll be more aware of what you're body is telling you.

> *Explain please.*

Your body is a storehouse of data. You store in it your experiences. And your body does talk to you. Don't you say, "I have a gut feeling," or "This problem is giving me a headache" or "This situation is making my body tense"? Don't you ache after a stressful meeting? Your body was storing the experience. Next time, when you have a similar problem, your body will react to the experience with a "gut feeling," a headache, a tension in your voice. Your body is communicating your past experiences. Thus, pay attention to your body. Respect it and trust it. You really have made a good decision only when your body feels relaxed. If you are tense, if it "does not smell good," if it "feels rotten," even if all the numbers show that you should do it and the lawyers assure you that you got a good deal...

> *Don't do it.*

You got it. Think, analyze, but at the end, listen to your intuition by listening to your body. You can also communicate better by watching the people you are talking to. Watching their eyes, eyebrows, and hand movements.

Watch their body and synchronize what they say with how they say it. You can't do that if you are preoccupied with your own body pains. If the parties in a meeting are relaxed, they communicate, that is, they understand each other better than if they are in pain; so slow down to get a fast result!

> *Okay. I understand although I believe I am going to look weird next time I start a meeting with "Ladies and gentlemen, please take a deep breath and relax!!!"*

You will get a weird reaction the first time around. Next time, they will ask for it. Try it...

> *So what's next?*

Go to the agenda and start with the first item, and watch the *(A)'s* eyes. This is very important. The moment the eyes go wandering, the *(A)* is thinking about the repercussions of your idea. Stop talking. I know this is very difficult for an *(E)*, but you must wait for the *(A)* to finish processing the information. Wait for the *(A)* to return from his or her wanderings.

> *What should I do in the meantime? Just sit there?*

If you are an *(E)*, you usually have many other ideas you want to present. While the *(A)* is thinking, you could make a list of those ideas. You should always have a pad of paper and a pen while in a meeting. If you don't write those ideas down, you'll worry that you might forget them later. That will cause you to keep talking when you should be quiet. If you know that you can find those ideas anytime, you won't feel so hard–pressed to say everything at once and send the poor *(A)* into a daze.

> *When the (A) comes back from deep thoughts, won't he or she have questions?*

The questions will most likely be about implementation. An *(E)* will probably get upset and think, "I can't believe this. I am trying to make millions of dollars and this pain in the neck is bugging me about insignificant details." *(E)s* often think *(A)s* are denying heavenly light because they can't find a candle.

Yes, this can drive (E)s insane.

First, don't get upset. Do not resist a style that is different from yours. Learn to recognize it and accept it. Then you can deal with it. What you should do is acknowledge the question. Say, "Good question. Let me write it down." Maybe you could write it on a flip chart, so the *(A)* can see that you are not ignoring the question. Say, "Let's address this later, Okay? After we finish the report we'll deal in detail with the questions. If you have any more questions, please write them down and we'll definitely address them." This way you are acknowledging the *(A)*'s concerns, yet you don't get side-tracked. Acknowledge all the questions but don't discuss them. Continue presenting the big picture, and when you are finished, summarize and say, "All right. Now let's look at the questions." In other words, you have to understand together the *what* and *why* before addressing the *how*. As you discuss the questions, you might find that the *(A)* was right to raise them. Some questions about implementation can justifiably negate your wonderful idea. But the *(A)* should not negate the idea before understanding it. You should not discuss the *how* until you have jointly understood the *what* and the *why*. You can't start with *what not* until you jointly understand the *what yes*. You can't all talk about cost until you all understand the value, because cost is not in a vacuum, but is relative to value.

How long should you stay in a meeting with an (A)?

Stay only the length of time you agreed upon. Don't say, "Please, ten more minutes and we will finish." First, there is a good chance it's not going to be ten minutes, but at least a half an hour. By that time the *(A)* will be furious. He has a schedule to live by. If you cannot finish in ten minutes, you will have to rush, and the worst mistakes in judgment are usually made in the last ten minutes of an extended meeting when people rush and are stressed.

But the (E) won't like this procedure. To stop on time... I mean you are asking a fish to fly.

Some fish do. And some birds dive under water. I'm not asking you to do what you like, but what you need to do. Do you think the bird goes under water for fun? It's going to feed. As for being difficult, my friend, management is selling ideas to others. You know how difficult it is to sell your own ideas to yourself. Imagine how much more difficult it is to sell them to others.

Are there other considerations when you deal with an (A)?

Yes, many. This conversation is just to get you started on the subject. For instance, to *(E)s*, numbers don't have to be exact; they're only a way to express a degree of magnitude. An *(E)* might say, "We sold a million." The fact is we sold somewhere between half a million and one and a half million. A million for *(E)s* is a more–or–less number.

Now for *(A)s*, 999,999 is not a million. That's why *(A)s* usually don't trust *(E)s*, and many *(E)s* get accused of lying. *(E)s* must be careful not to confuse ideas with facts, because *(A)s* take people literally. When *(A)s* catch you in a mistake, no matter how small, they no longer trust anything you say.

Enough about (A)s. I don't really like them anyway.

Watch your attitude. They'll keep you out of trouble. The bigger the *(E)* is in your *(PAEI)* code, the bigger the *(A)* you should seek. Success is a complementary team based on mutual respect. That means accepting each other's styles as legitimate.

You're right. I just have to remember that this is work, not a social club. Okay. Now how do you handle (E)s?

Well, we already know *(E)s* resist any idea unless it is theirs. So before meeting with an *(E)*, you have to think about how to make your idea appear to be the *(E)'s* idea.

You can walk in and say, "Here is problem X, the solution should be Y. Here it is, worked out to the last detail. I'm just asking for your approval." That's how you succeeded with the *(A)*. Is *(E)* going to like that?

No. In fact, the (E) would probably say, "Wrong problem, wrong solution." Looking for a hole in your reasoning, the (E) will attack the diagnosis. The (E) will try to find out what's wrong in an effort to put his or her own stamp on the solution. Finalized plans, in which there is nothing left for the (E) to contribute, will not be acceptable.

For *(E)s*, the *(A)* approach means you are taking charge and leaving them behind. You're ignoring them by not consulting with them. They feel disrespected. They are going to find a way to put you in your place sooner or later. If you ignore them, they are going to make you notice them, and notice them big.

Then how should I approach (E)s?

Don't ever go to them with a "final" solution to a problem. Don't ever expect them simply to agree with you. You must leave the whole issue open ended. Say "May I suggest..." "I've been thinking..." "It appears that..." "What do you think?" Let them put their stamp on your idea. And you should treat all *(E)* people like this, not only your *(E)* boss. I'm also talking about dealing with employees who are *(E)s*. They'll hate your telling them what to do, how to do it, and when you want it done. Why? Because you're not letting them use their brain. The *(E)s* want to contribute and you won't let them.

Use their creativity. Talk to them in their own language. Ask them, What do you think? What would you suggest? How can you help improve this? Enlist them so that they will own the idea.

Thank you. This is helpful. How do you deal with (I)s? What are (I)ntegrators or, in extreme cases, Super Followers or Soaped Fish looking for?

Why don't you try to answer that?

They're looking for agreement. They want political consensus.

If you tell an *(I)*, "The problem is this and the solution is that. We want your approval," what will he or she say?

"It's not time yet. We're not ready. Have you talked to Rudy? Have you talked to Paul? Have you talked to Denise?" An (I)ntegrator is going to ask questions to assess the political climate—the degree of consensus already available.

So, before you go to the (I)ntegrator...

You have to cover all your bases. You have to talk to Rudy and Paul and Denise to find out where they stand. You have to (I)ntegrate them first.

Then say to the (I)ntegrator, "We have a problem. All of us have discussed it. We agree on the solution, and we want your approval." The (I) will immediately ask, "What about Joe?" If you didn't talk to Joe, who is apparently important on the political map and you should have known that, the (I)ntegrator will say, "Well, I don't think we're ready yet." But if you say, "We talked to Joe and he is totally behind it," and you did get all the necessary people to buy into it,, the (I)ntegrator will say, "Well, what are we waiting for? Let's go!" Before giving their blessing, (I)ntegrators will go down the list of important people to make sure everyone is behind an idea. They understand capi intuitively.

What happens if I misread the person I'm talking to?

Your strategy will backfire. Just imagine you're an *(I)* talking to an *(E)* boss, and you treat him or her as another *(I)*. All your life you have tried to resolve conflicts and be sensitive to people. You talk to all the people affected by the problem or the solution. You resolve all the conflicts and integrate everyone. Then you go to your *(E)* boss and say, "We had this problem. We all met and agreed what the problem is, and we all agreed on the solution. We just want your agreement on it." What do you think? How will the *(E)* boss react?

He or she would probably sweat, thinking, "My God! There's been a coup d'etat behind my back. No one told me about the problem. They just got together and caucused against me. They have a solution and now they are backing me into a corner to approve it." The (E) will look for the first opportunity to fire the (I).

Management theory virtually ignores differences in style, while *(P)s* plan differently from *(A)s, (E)s,* or *(I)s*. Different people motivate, organize, and discipline differently. You *must* pay attention to the differences. You must deal with people according to their styles. Everyone has a different way of looking at the world, and that's why everyone wants to be treated differently. This has implications for designing reward systems, hiring people, promoting, evaluating performances, how we treat our children and should treat our spouse. It impacts how we should treat each other. Period.

It has implications for advertising as well. One way to look at market segmentation is through demographics: education, sex, geographical location, and so forth. Another way to look at it, I suggest, is through personality traits. This *(PAEI)* methodology has been used by many advertising agencies to appeal to different people in different ways.

The (P)roducing types, for instance, look for the functionality of a product. Let's take a car for example. The advertising directed at *(P)s* should focus on gas mileage, legroom, trunk space, and seating capacity.

The advertising aimed at *(A)s* should stress the warranty, repair record, and resale value.

For *(E)s*, facts like resale value and gas mileage are boring. *(E)s* probably look at what the car symbolizes. Implied sex attracts the *(E)s'* attention. Why else would anyone pay a hundred thousand dollars for a Ferrari? It's very difficult to sit inside one, and you can't drive 150 miles an hour in the city. But the idea of the sexy car and what it communicates to others is its main appeal. The car is a means to achieve the goals of the *(E)s'* fruitful imagination. It is not just a means of transportation as it is for a *(P)* or a good return on investment like it is for an *(A)*.

That's why when selling to *(E)s*, the colors, music, and images are very important. Sometimes it's difficult even to identify the product. The total image is being sold.

Wait. This explains something. Creative directors in advertising agencies are usually (E)s so they create advertisements they like. If they present such ideas to the vice presidents of an aging organization who are (A)s, they'll kick them out in mid–presentation.

Smart account executives in advertising have to know how to differentiate between clients and customers, the end users.

What about selling to (I)s?

To *(I)s* you're selling the affiliation. The advertisements for Rolex watches are a good example. The ad refers constantly to the fact that world leaders wear the watch. The message is that if you want to be identified with these people, you should wear the same watch. It's a symbol of belonging.

Good advertising campaigns have messages hitting all four *(PAEI)* market segments, or four separate campaigns aimed at the different segments.

Would you summarize all this?

To communicate successfully requires skill because different people understand the same words differently. They also have different needs to be satisfied. You must pay attention to those styles and needs if you want to sell your ideas.

> *Wait a minute! There's a complication here. Nobody is ever a perfect or exclusive type. We usually behave differently under different conditions or in interacting with different people. In reality we have different (PAEI) styles. What then?*

People must be sensitive. They should try one approach, and if they are not being understood, try another approach. They should always keep their eye on the people to whom they are selling ideas. They should adapt and change their style until the targeted people fully understand. All people must speak the four *(PAEI)* languages to some degree if they want to communicate well. That's why good managers must have well–rounded styles and why traveling abroad and getting to know different cultures is an important part of a person's education.

> *But now I feel as though I can never relax. I'll have to watch to whom I'm speaking and how I'm speaking. This makes me tense.*

Luckily, you don't have to do it all the time—only when there is conflict— only when you don't easily understand another person.

> *The problem is that at that time I'm least able to watch my style and adapt it to the person I'm trying to relate to.*

Yes. Whenever people are tired or upset, they usually start behaving in their own style and ignore the needs of the people they're talking to.

> *Then whenever people attend important meetings, it's extremely important that they be relaxed and well rested.*

Some people even meditate and fast before crucial meetings.

> *Are you serious?*

And there are times when people should stop a meeting altogether and reschedule it.

When?

When they're heading toward a breakdown. Think of it this way. Let's say you're very familiar with the workings of a certain machine, such as your car. You know the normal humming sound the engine makes. So if someone unfamiliar with your car asks what that noise is, you can say, "Oh, nothing. It's normal."

And once you know what a normal noise is, you can identify noises that aren't normal and indicate a breakdown. What should you do when you hear such noises?

Stop the engine immediately.

Absolutely. The same is true in personal relationships. Sometimes a conflict is normal and nothing to worry about. It's even music to your ears because you know you are both learning. It's pain with gain! But when you hear abnormal noise, you intervene.

How do you know what is normal and abnormal in conflicts?

Each of the *(PAEI)* styles has a typical abnormal noise, called "backup behavior." It appears when people aren't listening to or learning from each other anymore. It usually starts when people feel intimidated and fear they are losing control.

I bet it starts when they lose mutual trust and respect.

Yes, and the danger is that if they don't stop the discussion, it will be like a machine breaking down. It will keep sputtering until major and sometimes irreparable damage is done. What is breaking down is mutual trust and respect.

What are those typical backup patterns?

When *(P)s* feel they are losing control, they become little dictators. They proclaim, "That's it. I've heard enough! Here is what we're going to do and that's it. Period!"

(A)s usually freeze. They become very quiet. Their jaws lock. They don't look at you, but through you. They ignore you and pursue their own agenda. In Hebrew there is a military expression that describes this behavior: "The dogs are barking; the convoy keeps moving."

What is backup behavior for (I)s?

They yield. "Oh, that's what you mean? No problem. Fine. Don't worry." They sway with the wind, especially when it's blowing hard.

The most dangerous backup behavior is that of (E)s. If they feel they are losing control...

They attack. I know. They go for the throat. They cut you to pieces and destroy your self respect by publicly demeaning you.

Then they forget the whole thing. Right? They "kill" you, and the next morning act as if nothing happened.

But (A)s never forget. They keep a detailed diary in their minds, and sometimes on paper.

This sort of conflict occurs in many marriages. *(E)s* marry *(A)s* because they are complementary. Traditionally the *(E)* is the male and the *(A)* is the female. He attacks her, and she withstands it silently while mentally cataloging it. Years later, when she wants a divorce, he falls to pieces because he doesn't have a clue what happened and why. Then she starts reminding him what happened on that infamous afternoon ten years ago. He is shocked because he has very little memory of the fight. He hardly remembers what he had for breakfast, much less what happened ten years ago. But she never forgets and never forgives.

You just explained something very painful for me. Being a big, big (E), I easily revert to backup behavior. I am arrogant and show my displeasure easily. The other person, an (A), closes down because she feels threatened. Once I realize she is ignoring me, which is the worst thing that can happen to an (E), I get infuriated beyond

*belief. I feel threatened and upset, and I escalate my attack. And
the more I attack, the more she closes down. I am in pieces while
she freezes her emotions.*

Right! And she is in as much pain as you, only she shows it differently.

So what should we do?

Whoever is more in control of his or her emotions, even by a little bit, has to
stop the discussion the instant backup behavior is sensed. Immediately.
And you should not resume the discussion too soon either. What did you
do with the machine that sounded as if it were breaking down? You
stopped it. Should you just start it again?

No. You should check the source of the breakdown first.

The same holds for personal conflict. After you have stopped the discussion and cooled off, you should find out what caused the other party to feel
threatened. Clear up that issue before continuing the discussion.

When you notice backup behavior in a heated business meeting, say
something like, "Let's discuss it tomorrow. I hear you and I want to give
you the full attention you deserve. I am too emotional right now." Refuse to
continue the discussion. *(P)s* and *(E)s* will get upset and insist the problem
be resolved. They hate pain and want to get it over with. When they hear
abnormal noise, they don't slow the machine down; they speed it up. Don't
get sucked in. The next day, start off by asking, "What happened yesterday?
You seemed upset. What did I say or what happened that upset you?" Try
to find out what it was. Only when that issue is resolved should you
reactivate the machine. Then you can go back to discuss the issue you were
dealing with.

This requires a lot of self–discipline.

Success is not just talent. Talent alone does not mean success. Fast in, fast
out! You will burn out in no time. For producing results, the more talent
you have, the more self–discipline you must have.

And self–discipline alone is barren.

Absolutely. You need *both* talent and self–discipline. Analyze the people who have been successful in any field—sports, arts, business, politics, any field whatsoever—and you will find equal amounts of talent and self–discipline.

Let's exercise some self–discipline now and stop this conversation. I am hungry and tired. Let's get together again tomorrow .

I noticed you always say, "I am hungry and tired." They seem to go together with you. When you get tired, you get hungry, as if you believe food will give you strength. Perhaps if you were less tired and more relaxed, you would eat less. Don't diet. Relax.

There you go again. See you soon.

Conversation 13

Perceiving Reality

So far we've said that different people not only behave differently, they think differently. If you want to sell your ideas to people, you have to think as they do and communicate in a "language" they understand.

People process information and come to conclusions at different speeds. People have different priorities in decision making. Even the same words have different meanings to different people. Today we're going to talk about how to avoid the miscommunication that stems from differences in perceptions.

May I first ask how you learned what you are teaching me now?

That's a good question. You don't learn only from teachers or books. You also learn from rocks, flowers, and children. I learned about perceptions from my kids when they were toddlers. The older, Topaz, was in his high chair banging his spoon and splattering food all over the place when he suddenly pointed at something and shouted, "Mine!"

I was puzzled as to why my son was developing capitalistic tendencies so early in life. Why was he so materialistic, so possessive? What was going on with his upbringing? Why wasn't his first word "love" or "give"?

Then my second son, Shoham, did the same thing at about the same age, fifteen months or so later.

Years later, while lecturing around the world, I learned that children shout "Mine" at about the same age in all countries and in all languages. I wondered why.

After working for years in changing organizational cultures, I realized grown–ups are nothing more than grown–up children. They too shout "Mine" all the time. After years of observation, I had the following illumination.

A situation can be perceived in three different ways, or in any combination of the three. If you look at this diagram I've drawn, you'll see three circles labeled *is*, *want*, and *should*.

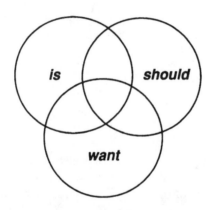

The first perception of reality is the *is*. It's the present reality. It's right now. For instance, you are listening to me right now. However, *is* is not necessarily what *should* be, which is the second perception. Maybe as you *are* listening to me, it crossed your mind that you *should* be working or doing something else now. Maybe you *should* be with your kids. Some little voice in the back of your mind is telling you what you *should* be doing, rather than what you *are* doing.

The third perception is what you *want* to be doing. While you *are* listening to me and thinking you *should* be in the office, you really *want* to go on vacation.

This sounds like a lot of internal conflict.

It is. It's what you *are* doing versus what you believe you *should* be doing versus what you *want* to be doing. And that causes pain.

Where is "mine"?

It is where the three circles overlap. What *is* happening *should* be happening, and you *want* it to happen. When children shout "Mine" they're not being possessive. They're really saying, "I *want* that." Children don't know the difference between *want, should,* and *is.* So they're really saying, "Since I *want* it, it *should* be, and it *is.*"

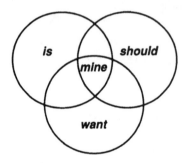

In the first five or six years of their lives, children cry a lot because they're learning to differentiate between the three perceptions. If you tell toddlers, "Don't touch the oven; it's hot," what do they do the moment you turn your back?

Touch the oven!

And get burnt and cry. They are starting to learn the difference between the *want* and the *is.* When Topaz was very little, he stood in front of a wall and said, "Move." Then he cried when the wall didn't move.

If you tell children, "It *is* ten o'clock; you *should* go to sleep because you have school tomorrow," what do they say? "I don't *want* to go to sleep." And they start carrying on. They are learning to differentiate between *want* and *should.* They are learning to act according to the *should* and not exclusively by the *want.*

As a matter of fact, we send kids to school to learn what they *should* do. If they have been thoroughly deprived of *want* after years of learning the *should*, they rebel simply to stay sane!

When we grow up and experience a mid–life crisis, we realize that the *should* and the *want* are not that crucial. What is very relevant is the *is*. We learn to live with reality. If we succeed in learning to appreciate the *is*, we enjoy the best time of our life. We finally learn what we like and still have time to enjoy it. We put aside the *shoulds and wants*. We like the *is*, and enjoy the now.

But the best is to be in the state of "mine." Right?

Yes, and a way to see *mine* as happiness is when we are in love or, in this case, rather, infatuated. We say to the person, "You are mine." What we are really saying is, "What you *are*, what you *should* be, and what I *want* you to be are one and the same. You are perfect." But I don't call that true love. I call that "adolescent love" or "temporary madness."

Temporary madness?

Yes, because after we get married, we discover that what *is*, *should not* be, and what *should* be, we don't necessarily *want*, and what we *want, isn't*. To maintain a working relationship we have to learn to live with reality, and in the process, we suffer pain. That's how we move from the overlapping core of teenage love to mature love, which means accepting reality and imperfection.

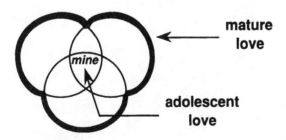

The French differentiate between loving and liking this way: You like because of; you love in spite of.

That's good. In some societies people don't marry out of love. They do not expect the three circles to overlap and be *mine*. They marry as a commitment, not out of some infatuation. In these societies the man and woman who are marrying don't even see each other until the wedding. Today we expect *mine* to be continuous. When we don't continually experience it, we get upset, we experience pain driven by unfulfilled expectations, and we ask for a divorce. Rabbi Kushner, the author of *When Bad Things Happen to Good People*[11], said in one of his lectures that a modern couple asked him to officiate at their wedding, except they wanted to change the vows. Instead of saying "until death do us part," they wanted to say something like "for as long as we love each other." How about that? In this case, is there a commitment to nurture love regardless, or is there an expectation to benefit from love regardless?

Mine does not equal love. It equals immature love. Mature love is present when we accept and love our partner "in spite of." When we accept our own imperfections first, we can accept the imperfections of others. And love of others starts with love of oneself. You have to forgive yourself before you can forgive others. Thus love grows from the inside out, not from the outside in. No one can give it to you. You give it to yourself by giving it to others.

But how about relating this to management? What will happen when we are not in the core where the three circles overlap?

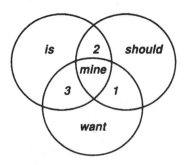

Let's look at the place on the diagram where I have entered the number 1. This is an area where what we *want should* be, but it *isn't*. It creates frustration. I *want* certain people to behave in a certain disciplined way in my company and they *should* behave that way. As an example, we *should*

have budgetary controls, and I *want* budgetary controls. It upsets me that we don't have them. The reality *isn't* what I *want* and what I believe *should* be; that frustrates me. I might even get hostile and fire some people.

Another frustration is in area 2. In this case what *should* be actually *is*, although we don't *want* it to be that way. For instance, say you are denied a loan, and looking at your financial statement, it *is* not surprising you were denied one. You *should* be denied the loan because your financial situation *is* not stable. However, you *want* the loan. You don't want to accept what actually *is* and what *should* happen. You don't *want* it to actually happen. So, you go home frustrated. It *is* painful to accept rejection, no matter how justified it is.

I call area number 3 "living in sin." You do what you *want*, although you know you *shouldn't*. For instance, you know you *shouldn't* smoke but you do it anyway. Why are you doing it? Because you *want* to.

Wait. How, specifically, does this relate to management?

First, I claim that people confuse the *is*, *want*, and *should*. Look at some of our political writings. "All men *are* created equal." Aren't we confusing the *is* with the *want* and *should*? *Are* people born equal or *should* they be born equal or do we *want* them to be born equal? Another example: "America *is* the leader of the free world." *Is* it? *Should* it be? Or do we *want* it to be?

But why this confusion?

Because people with different *(PAEI)* styles perceive reality differently.

For instance, which tendency do (E)ntrepreneurial types exhibit? Do they come from the *want*, *should*, or *is?*

They come from the want.

They confuse *want* with what *is*. Their style is "Since I *want* it, it *is*." That's why typical *(E)s* will say, "We sold a million dollars worth of goods." And the *(A)s* will ask, "Where's the contract?" *(E)s* answer, "Well, the client is meeting next week to decide."

Do you see what just happened? The *(E)s* confuse the *want* with the *is*. "Since I *want* it, it *is*." Also, they might say, "We *are* the leaders of our industry." *Are* we, or *should* we be, or do we *want* to be?

Yes, you are right. It reminds me of a manager who said at a meeting, "We are the best company in the industry." When she was challenged, she said, "Well, we have all the ingredients to be the best."

If you study history, you will find many examples of wars conducted with this confusion. Many people died because the leader was a dictatorial *(E)* who operated exclusively on the *want* perception, ignoring *is* and subordinating the *should* to serve the *want* exclusively.

An example?

Hitler, towards the end of World War II, for instance. He was conducting the war on the map of Europe using fingers to measure distances, ignoring reality, and executing the messengers who communicated the bad news of that reality.

And who perceives that since it should be, it is?

(A)s. If you ask an *(A)*, "Do we have a solution to this problem?" He or she might say, "Yes, we do! We spent a million dollars on it, didn't we?" You might challenge that statement by saying, "Wait a minute! I know we *should* have a solution because we spent a million dollars, but that's not the question. *Do* we have a solution?" When do we have a solution? Only if it works.

Now tell me, which type perceives what *is* as *is* ?

The (P)s, the (P)roducers. What is, is. Never mind the want and the should.

Yes, and who is continuously "dancing" around so that you can't figure out if what they believe *is*, or what they *want* or what they believe *should* be?

The (I)s.

(I)s are capable of understanding the differences and what different people are saying because they don't really have an exclusive process by which they come to reality. At the same time, they do not reveal their thoughts, since they want to read yours first. They understand what *is* differently.

That can create a lot of confusion.

The confusion stems from the fact that different people perceive the world differently, as we've discussed several times already.

An *(E)* comes to a meeting and says, "We sold a million dollars."

The *(A)* responds, "Where's the contract?"

The *(E)* says, "We're going to get the contract next week after they decide."

"Aha!" says the *(A)*, "Then we don't have a contract."

"Yes, but we *should* have the contract soon. They like our product. They're going to sign."

"But we *don't* have it signed yet."

"Yes, but we *will*," says the *(E)*, who is shouting by now.

"But we don't have it in our hands yet," says the *(A)*.

"What the hell is the difference? Why are you so pedantic? Just to needle me or what?"

"You must be kidding," says the *(A)*. "You give me half–truths. When I try to get to the bottom of things, you get mad and accuse me of persecuting you!"

The *(I)* intervenes and says, "Now let's talk this over. What is the problem?"

While this goes on, the *(P)* gets very upset. "Listen guys! Do we have a contract or don't we? What the hell is going on?" The *(P)* just wants to finish the meeting, get back to work and avoid this interpersonal nonsense. "Shape up or ship out! " That's the *(P)* attitude.

How does understanding the differences in perception help you?

Whenever I conduct meetings with companies which I'm coaching to Prime, I insist that the words *is, want,* and *should* be used in the *(P)* sense. So if people say, "We *are* the leaders of the industry," they had better be speaking in *(P)* language. If they are not the leaders, I expect people in a meeting to say, "We *want* to be the leaders of the industry, but we *are* not yet. What we *should* do in order to become the leader is ..." Do you see how I'm using the words now?

If you sit in a meeting and listen carefully to the way people talk, you'll find they continually confuse *is, want,* and *should*. Instead of saying, "I *want* something," which is arrogant and uncomfortable to say, they say, "We *should* do that." When you analyze what they said, you will find that what they really meant is that they *want* to do it. So I insist that they say *want* instead of *should*. *Should* is reserved for those things that must be done because the situation dictates it. *Should* has nothing to do with what you *want*.

Is there a particular sequence for using the three perceptions?

Yes.

Which one should we use first?

It's like having three lenses for your camera, each lens a different color. But these are special lenses. The sequence in which you put them on determines the color of the picture you get. Let's assume that each of the three perceptions is a different lens: an *is* lens, a *want* lens and a *should* lens.

Planning should start with *want*. Planning can't be successful without dreaming. You have to have a vision. As George Bernard Shaw once wrote, "The reasonable man adapts himself to the world. The unreasonable one persists in trying to adapt the world to himself. Therefore all progress depends on the unreasonable man."

If you continue too long with unreasonable dreaming, insisting on something that does not and cannot ever work, it can become a nightmare. Somebody has to wake up and say, "All right, what is the reality? I know what we *want*, but *should* we do that?" *Should* comes after the *want*. We have to put on the *should* lens to move from utopian dreams to economically achievable goals. We have to look at the cost factors and trade–offs. "Here is what we want. Now let's start looking at the constraints. How much is this dream going to cost us? Finally, if we *should* do what we *want* to do, let's go and make the new reality, the new *is*, happen." The sequence for planning is if we *want* it, and if it *should* be, then it *is* going to be.

Want ⟶ Should ⟶ Is

What if our plan is not working. We are continually deviating from it. What should the sequence be now?

You cannot stay in the same sequence. If you say, "I'm ignoring that it *is* not working at all, but I *want* it nevertheless," you're a spoiled brat. Some *(E)s*, when they are Arsonists, are spoiled brats. They ignore reality.

That's how (E)s sometimes destroy what they've built. They stay attached to their big enterprise and the dream it represents. They're not willing to budge. They refuse to change. Refusing to wake up. And as they refuse to recognize that it's not working, they lose, piece by piece, what they worked so hard to build.

They refuse to recognize what *is*. They refuse to accept reality. They cling to the *want* perception exclusively. "I *want* it. Since I *want* it, it *should* be. And since it *should* be, it had better *be*," although it *isn't*!

The way to make change is to first accept reality. The way to move on is to accept where you are. As long as you fight your present, you won't have the energy to move toward the future. Once you accept reality, all your energy is available to make change. Thus the change sequence must start with *is*. What *is*, *is*. Now, in light of what *is*, you can ask what do we *want* to do and then, what *should* we do. The sequence for changing a situation should be   *is* —> *want* —> *should*, while for planning it is *want* —> *should* —> *is*. If you confuse the sequences, you're a fanatic. The philosopher George Santayana said that a fanatic, having misunderstood what the reality is, doubles and triples and quadruples his efforts. That's how he gets stuck deeper and deeper in the sand.

No change is possible without accepting reality first. For instance, you are not going to lose weight until you admit you're overweight. Fighting your weight will only add to it.

From what I understand of Arsonists, they have a hard time accepting reality.

They do. They cling to dreams even after they become nightmares. They refuse to wake up. Often, they wait and actually *rely* on miracles. They do not change direction easily.

But you told me they change direction all the time, remember? The big wheel turns back and forth while the little wheels get ground to dust.

Life is not linear: left on the left and right on the right. If you keep going right you will end up on the left. The Earth is not flat, it's round

The same is true for love versus hate, hot versus cold, and change versus stability. Nothing can be more permanent than a continuous temporary. If you have a fever, you feel cold. If you love someone very, very much, you hate him or her from time to time.

Have you looked at wheels turning very fast? They appear to stay in one place. *(E)s* change everything except change itself, so the more things change, at a certain point, they don't change. *(E)s* believe they make strategic decisions while at best their decisions have only a tactical impact. Too much change has the impact of no change. It is a continuous mess.

Okay. Now let's take a break.

Done!

Conversation 14

How to Convert Committee Work into Teamwork

So far we have said that conflict is necessary because we need a complementary team and a commonality of interests. To make this conflict functional, we need mature people who communicate and recognize the differences between people's decision–making style, the right organizational structure, and the right decision–making process.

We've discussed the people factor. As to the decision–making process, it has three parts. The first is how to have an effective dialogue; the second is how to handle the different perceptions, which we talked about in our last conversation. Now we will cover the third part, which is how to manage meetings.

Can you tell me again how you discovered this material?

Once I was invited to lecture in Canada. The chief executive officer of the host company picked me up at the airport the evening before the lecture, and then invited me to a hospitality suite to meet the other executives attending the program. They were playing poker. There were three tables with four executives at each one. They joked and laughed; their energy was high. Hundreds of dollars changed hands. It was well past midnight when they finally stopped playing.

As they were leaving, I noticed something very interesting. At four o'clock in the morning, after playing poker all night, their adrenaline was still flowing. Several said, "Great game! Let's get together again soon."

I wondered about what had happened. If I had taken those same executives and put them in a meeting where they would have to make decisions, they would've been exhausted after two hours, drained of energy. None of them would look forward to the next committee meeting.

Seeing this exhilaration, I wondered about the difference between playing poker and attending a committee meeting. If the same executives were given a group assignment to make a decision, why wouldn't they behave the same way they did in the poker game? That poker game inspired me to write training programs on participatory management by teamwork, rather than by committee. Now tell me, what's the difference between playing cards and conducting management by committee?

They were playing, having fun.

Fun is the outcome, not the cause. The difference is not that people like games. Most executives like to manage too. They like to make decisions.

They like the challenge in poker.

They compete in business as well. That's certainly a challenge.

They all start with an equal chance?

True, but you could say the same in business as well.

Rules! The game has explicit rules.

Right. You wouldn't play poker or any other game with people who violate the rules. You wouldn't trust them. All games have rules. When children make up games, the first thing they do is agree upon the rules. If someone breaks the rules, they stop playing and fight. Any interdependence in life is governed by rules. We just have to discover them. There is no functional interdependence without rules of conduct, although we aren't always aware of, nor do we always understand them. What disrupts a functional interdependence is called a disease or a problem, and that occurs when we knowingly or unknowingly break some rules.

When we visit a foreign country and do something contrary to that culture, we realize we have to learn the rituals, which are really the rules of that culture. Life, my friend, is one long game, and you had better know the rules.

Knowing is not the problem. It's learning them that's difficult because they change constantly.

And more rapidly every year.

So where does this take us? Why is knowing the rules and playing by them so important?

Because there is no teamwork without mutual respect and trust. And there is no mutual respect and trust without adherence to mutually agreed–upon rules of conduct.

If that's true, then following the appropriate rules will also make teamwork happen.

Now you understand. So here's what I did. I applied (A)dministration to (I)ntegration. First, I realized that anything that is disrespectful or fosters mistrust must be forbidden, and everything that strengthens trust and respect must be encouraged.

And that is the bottom line?

Yes. Rules that foster respect and trust!

But what does respect mean? How do you generate respect by making rules?

I found the answer in the work of philosopher Immanuel Kant. He said that respect is the acceptance of the sovereignty of the other party.

What does sovereignty mean in this case?

Think of what it means in international relations.

It means that a nation has the legitimate freedom to do what it wants regarding its own internal matters.

Right, and if it makes a decision about its internal matters we don't like, we can't send our army to force that nation to change its decision. We would violate its sovereignty.

Right.

Well, the same applies to interpersonal relations. I accept your sovereignty to think and speak differently because that is your own internal matter. You have not affected me; I respect you. The day I say, "How dare you think or say that? That is the most insane thing I have ever heard in my life," what have I done? I have sent out my air force to bombard you to change your mind, although all you really did was express your thoughts. Your thoughts and their expression weren't an action against me and didn't affect me at all.

Yes. Voltaire is credited with saying, "I disapprove of what you say, but I will defend to the death your right to say it." Mutual respect means, then, that we accept each other's sovereignty to think and express ourselves differently.

Right.

How about mutual trust?

I am working on that one. So far it seems that the bottom line is: "Do unto others as you would want done unto you."

But that was precisely the wrong thing in mutual respect, in communication. Remember?

Yes, I know. We need united differences and synchronized differences; we need harmony—not in spite of but because of differences. If the rules are not followed correctly, we can get unity that kills the difference or differences that kill the unity.

I am confused and feel uncomfortable about this explanation.

Me too. I am still working on it and who knows how long it will take. But this gives you a glimpse of what I went through and am still going through, in order to get to what I've told you so far. It is very complicated to make things simple and very simple to make things complicated.

How about giving me some rules that you have tested and that do work to guide me through this maze?

I developed rules which I tested in many companies in different cultures around the world. I found people could change their behavior without *talking* about mutual trust and respect. If the structure of the organization changed, and people learned the rules of conduct that nourish mutual trust and respect, guess what? People naturally started acting with mutual trust and respect. I developed an experientially based behavior modification program, not a cognitive program, that tries to persuade people to change their attitudes through factual knowledge.

Could you give me some examples of those rules?

They are very simple, but their simplicity makes them powerful. I warn you not to discount their power just because they are simple.

Why are you warning me?

Because some people have been conditioned by the academic world to think that if something isn't complicated, it's too simple to work. Well, just the opposite is true. If it's not simple, then it's too complicated. I've spent years trying to simplify things, and believe me, that's hard work.

So tell me some simple, but powerful rules you've learned.

OK, I'll give you a sample. One rule deals with the starting time of meetings. Meetings don't usually start right on time. The few people who show up on time feel foolish. Important people will probably be late, and the more important they are, the later they believe they can arrive. You can often analyze the whole organizational hierarchy by the order in which people arrive for a meeting. The boss arrives last, and if anyone arrives later than that, it's offensive. The first rule in my methodology is that meetings start on time. This shows respect for everyone attending.

But what if it's impossible for someone to be on time?

That's okay. People may be up to ten minutes late as long as they pay an agreed–upon penalty for every minute of tardiness. They also may pay per incident—whatever is agreed upon. So latecomers pay their penalty and sit down. Paying the fine indicates they realize they've broken the rules. It is a symbolic act, not a financial punishment. No explanation for tardiness is necessary, regardless of how legitimate the excuse is. Payment is expected nevertheless.

That's a pretty radical rule. Give me another one.

Another rule deals with who speaks in the meeting. When people speak about some deep emotional problem or about something they've created, they usually keep thinking about what they've said even after they've stopped talking. They're listening to their own "tape," checking whether they've said what they wanted to say. When that happens, their eyes usually start wandering.

Now the danger is that, as they mentally listen to themselves, somebody else might start talking to them. But to whom are they still listening?

Obviously to themselves.

That's why it is very difficult to communicate, especially with *(E)s*. They are so creative and have many of their own ideas to listen to. The slightest provocation starts them thinking so intensely that they usually don't hear others. That's why they're often accused of being arrogant and disrespectful. It isn't out of disrespect that they don't listen; it's because they have so many of their own ideas to listen to.

When a person finishes speaking, the chairman usually passes the right to speak to somebody else. This procedure is a big mistake.

Why? Someone has to keep the meeting going.

When someone has stopped talking and another has started, the first person isn't listening to the next person. The first person is mentally reviewing his or her statements. And after several hours of discussing emotionally charged subjects, all the people in the meeting are listening to their own "tapes" and not to what others have said. They might *hear* each other, but they are not *listening* to each other .

How do we know when someone is finished talking?

You tell me. Who is the only person in the world who knows that you've finished saying what you wanted to say?

Me!

Right. Only the people speaking know when they have finished communicating. Here, then, is the second rule of the Adizes methodology: people may talk for as long as they wish. If they stop talking, think about what they have said, then resume talking, that's okay. No one else may interrupt. When they really feel they've finished talking, they look to their right. The moment they turn their head to the right, it signals to others who wish to talk that they may raise their hands. Then the person who has just finished speaking calls on the next person to his or her right who has a hand raised. Notice he or she doesn't call the person who raised a hand first, but the first person on his or her right who has a hand raised. And the person speaking must call the next person by first name only.

> *Why must they use first names only? Why not use the last name or just gesture to the right? Why not just say "pass" or nod, signifying permission to speak? This sounds terribly constraining. I thought you were an (E); now I think you're a closet (A).*

The only way you can evaluate what I am talking about is by experiencing it, not by analyzing it. Please understand—I have worked out the minutest details of how to convert an organization's culture from one that lacks trust and respect to one that has trust and respect. I did not stay with theory alone. Theory is nothing until it is tested.

This rule about addressing others by first name only was developed for many reasons. When you are emotionally involved with something, you might forget the name of the person you're talking to. It may take a few seconds before you can remember it. If you do remember it, that's a sign you have finished. If you have difficulty remembering, you haven't really finished thinking. Don't rush it. Go back and think about the issue again. Think about what you have said, restate it, and correct it as many times as necessary, until you're certain you have said what you wanted to say.

When you come back from your deep thoughts, turn to your right, and if you can instantly recall the first name of the person on your right with a hand raised, you have finished thinking and talking.

Why can't I use his last name?

There is a good reason for that. Remember when you were a child and your mother or father got upset with you? They would call you by your full name. "Jonathan Smith, it's time for you go to bed." That's how they made it formal. On the other hand, it's harder to be upset when you use a person's first name. This is your insurance policy against the group's becoming upset over a subject. If everyone has to call each other by first names, that will lower the level of frustration and hostility. Somebody might be very upset, and speak and speak and speak. When the time comes to pass the permission, that person will usually take a deep breath and say, "Joe." He will not be able to say "Joe!!!" in an aggressive way. The last name can be expressed in an aggressive way, as was done by our parents, but not the first name. That's the rule for keeping the climate friendly. Furthermore, people love to hear their first name mentioned. It reinforces a supportive climate, no matter how painful the discussion.

Why not pass to the first person who raised a hand?

Because then the *(P)s* will dominate the meeting. *(P)s* or *(E)s* will raise their hands first even though they haven't finished thinking about what they want to say. They will do that just to get the floor. They're going to present half–baked ideas. People in the meeting will start behaving aggressively as they compete for airtime.

By calling the first person on the right who has a hand raised, you create a situation in which others will simply have to wait.

Why is waiting so good? That's exactly why I hate meetings. They take forever.

In the Hebrew language, the words *tolerance, patience,* and *pain* all come from the same root. That made me think. What we want in teamwork is mutual respect. But there is no mutual respect without mutual tolerance, right?

Right.

I can't say, "I respect your opinions, but I don't tolerate them." That doesn't work. There is no respect without tolerance, and there is no tolerance without patience. I can't say, "I tolerate your different opinions, but I have no patience to hear them." The only way you can tolerate someone is to have patience.

Now, tolerating different opinions and developing the patience to hear them is painful.

I can see why so many people show disrespect in committee meetings. They cannot take the pain of being tolerant of people who disagree with them.

So what do people do when they have different opinions and there is little tolerance? They raise their voices and speak fast. You know what they're exhibiting? Pain! They rush through the meeting, trying to escape the pain. They are speeding headlong on the highway to destructive conflict.

Calling on the first person to the right who has a hand raised, even though others may have raised their hands first, forces the other people to wait. As they wait, they develop patience, and as they develop patience they develop tolerance. Slowly, they learn to live with pain. In my opinion, the purpose of management training and development is to increase a person's ability to handle the pain that stems from conflict.

Experienced managers know how to deal with the pain involved in dealing with people. They have weathered so many fires, they're like Teflon cookware. Nothing sticks to them anymore. Young people who can't sustain pain have difficulty managing because they lose their heads at the first twinge of discomfort. They go into backup behavior and misjudge. Experience is important, because it helps managers develop the ability to handle interpersonal pain.

In the Adizes methodology, we train people to become better managers partly by training them to tolerate the pain of listening to people who disagree with them. What happens is very interesting. Here's an example.

Let's say the seventh person down the circle raised a hand first. But the right to speak must be given to the first person to the speaker's right who has raised a hand. Let's say the right to speak is passed to several people before it is finally awarded to that seventh person. At first that person was fidgeting and anxious to speak, but by the time he or she is called on, he or she realizes, "I've nothing to say. I've changed my mind." While listening to the others, that person learned something. Mutual respect is developing here, because people are learning from each other.

You're saying that if we don't pass the right to speak to the person that raised a hand first, respect wouldn't develop?

Right. The *(E)s* and *(P)s*, who are fast on the draw, would dominate the meeting. The *(A)s* would take their time to think things over, and the *(I)s*, who always watch what's going on would never speak.

The *(E)s* would conclude that the *(A)s* and *(I)s* have nothing to contribute and would despise them. Instead of mutual respect, mutual disrespect would set in. By being forced to listen to *(A)s*, the *(E)s* might realize they aren't the only ones with good ideas.

The best sign that people are learning and that there is mutual respect is when people don't rush to make judgments. After you manage several meetings this way, you'll hear people say, "I have an idea, but I'm not so sure about it. I would like to hear other people's reactions." They have started listening to each other.

Would you go over these rules one more time?

First, whoever speaks may speak for as long as he needs. Nobody may speak or raise a hand while someone else is speaking. People must wait their turn—no rushing, no pressure. When a person finishes talking—and he is the only one who can make that decision—he looks to his right. Whoever wishes to talk should then raise a hand. The person who has finished talking calls on the first person to his right who raised a hand. He must address that next person by first name. The moment he calls the next person's first name, he relinquishes the right to speak. Now only the called upon person may speak.

But the person might talk forever. Some people have something to say, and there are others who have to say something. I could grow old listening to the latter type go on and on.

If you want to make conversations long, make them short. And if you want to make them short, you had better allow them to be long.

There you go again. What happens if people speak out of turn?

Anyone who interferes with the person who is speaking pays a penalty. The money collected for all violations is given to charity.

People know they're not supposed to violate rules when they see the penalty money pile up in front of them. They wait their turn, then speak softly. In Hebrew we say, "Divrey Hachamim benachat Nishmaim," which means "the words of wise people are listened to peacefully." Stupid people shout and scream at each other. In Arabic they say, "Al agial min alshiatan," meaning, "rushing is from the devil."

In meetings that are run according to these rules, you know that no one will interrupt, pressure, or override you. You can think fully about what you want to say. You have the chance to check whether you said what you meant to say, and you are always able to finish expressing your thoughts. This enables other people to hear you as well. In turns, we go around the circle until we have finished discussing whatever the issue is.

Yes, but what happens if one person speaks about subject X, then another talks about subject Y, and someone else starts with Q? Before you know it, you're talking about fifteen different subjects and have lost the original agenda.

That's why the chairman of the meeting, called the (I)ntegrator, must see to it that people don't change the agenda.

The (I)ntegrator must direct the discussion and interrupt the flow as necessary. By doing this the group will not spread itself out in several different directions.

What about the penalties? Do they always work?

Penalties don't work well with extreme *(E)*s. It doesn't work well in countries like Israel and Greece, where *(E)* is prevalent in the culture. In the United States it doesn't work well in young companies that are very (E)ntrepreneurial. Big *(E)*s don't care about money. I've seen more than one case where an *(E)* would get upset, throw ten dollars on the table and say, "Here is one dollar for violating the rule now, and nine dollars for the next nine times I want to speak. Because I want to speak when I want to."

(E)s wouldn't mind losing a hundred dollars in fines in one session as long as they could make their opinion heard. For *(E)s*, I have a different rule. Anytime *(E)s* violate the rules, they lose their turn to speak. There is no bigger punishment for *(E)s* than not being allowed to speak. So they quiet down, follow the rules, and participate like any other team member.

Are there more rules?

Many, many more.

Have you tested them?

I've developed a methodology that has been practiced for more than twenty years in hundreds of companies around the world. It's been validated in different cultures with different technologies and in companies of many different sizes. We have taken companies and converted them from cultures with low mutual trust and respect and low cooperation and communication to ones with strong mutual trust and respect and strong cooperation and communication. We have converted the energy that was being wasted on internal conflicts to energy that is now being directed externally to deal with competition and satisfy client needs.

Does it last?

It works. But it is not stable. If the companies stop practicing the Adizes methodology they will lose the advantage the methodology provides.

Why would they stop?

Because change, real change, is painful. Adizes is effective, but not popular, so some companies stop. For instance, if a new CEO comes in who is not trained in the methodology, he or she can stop the process, change the structure, and dismantle what was painstakingly built.

How long does it take to implement your system in an organization?

Changing an organization can take from one to three years, with one to three days of workshops every month.

> *Can you give me a fast Band–Aid? Give me the bottom of the bottom of the bottom line of your theory. What would you say if you had to say it while standing on one foot?*

Build a climate of mutual trust and respect in your organization by having 1) the right structure, 2) disciplined communication and decision making, and 3) mature people who command and grant respect and trust.

That is the essence. That's how you're going to build a better organization, or whatever it is you're managing, including your marriage, children, community, or your life.

> *These were very long conversations. How about summarizing them again?*

Summary

Management is the process for solving problems that emerge because of change. Those problems have a predictable pattern: some are normal, some are abnormal. They follow an organization's lifecycle as described in my book *Corporate Lifecycles*. In order to manage anything well, we must make quality decisions about how to solve these problems and we must be able to implement those decisions efficiently.

In order to make good decisions, a complementary team is necessary. None of us alone can make first–class decisions all the time. Furthermore, in order to implement decisions we need a perceived long–term commonality of interests with the people necessary to implement what has been decided.

Having a complementary team creates conflict. This happens because we miscommunicate when we think, speak and act differently. Commonality of interests is not a common occurrence either. We don't always have a win–win climate. It is another source of conflict.

Conflict is a natural part of the process of managing or living. Because management has to deal with change, no management exists without conflict. Different people think differently about what should be done about change. And different people have different interests that are affected by change. Show me change, and I'll show you conflict. The trick to managing change well is to convert the conflict from destructive to constructive.

Conflict is constructive and synergistic when people who are different from each other learn from each other's differences. Communication and mutual respect are necessary for this to happen.

If there is a perceived win–win climate, at least in the long run, and if we trust each other that short–term imbalances in interests will even out, we will cooperate, and conflicts of interest can be channeled into being constructive.

Therefore, *good management is teamwork based on mutual trust and respect, on cooperation and communication.*

For successful teamwork we need rules of conduct in the process of decision making that nourish respect and trust. We also need people who are mature and well balanced, and we need a correctly designed organizational structure.

Conflict *is* the reality that accompanies change. We *want* it to be constructive. For that we *should* have the right people, the right process of decision making, and the right organizational structure.

Thank you so much. We'll talk again another time. I am especially intrigued by the process of converting the destructive energy created by conflict into constructive energy.

I suggest you revisit these conversations occasionally. I assure you that you will understand things you did not understand the first time around. And that will be true for every successive visit. Also, try explaining these conversations to someone who has not read them yet. Through the discipline of explaining, you will discover important new things in those conversations you never noticed before.

> *In Serbo–Croatian, the word "to teach" is identical to the word "to relearn." When you teach you really find out how much you have learned, how much you know. Anyway, thank you for your time.*

Thank you for giving me your time and for being willing to hear what I have to say. What value is there to what I think, if there is no one with whom I can share it?

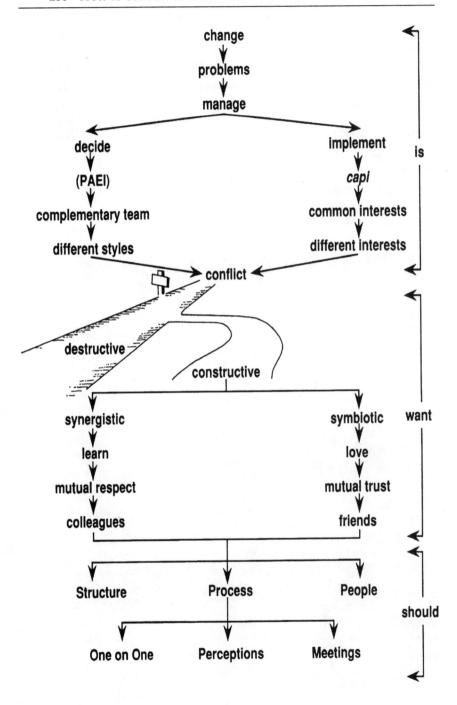

Endnotes

1   Ichak Adizes, "Beyond The Peter Principle," working paper, UCLA Graduate School of Management. Later published as "Mismanagement Styles," *California Management Review* 19: 5-20 (Winter 1976); then expanded and published as *How To Solve The Mismanagement Crisis* (Dow Jones/Irwin, 1979; reprinted, Santa Monica: Adizes Institute, 1980); further elaborated in *Corporate Lifecycles: How And Why Corporations Grow And Die and What To Do About It* (Englewood Cliffs: Prentice Hall, 1988).

2   Ichak Adizes, *Industrial Democracy: Yugoslav Style* (New York: Free Press, 1971; reprinted Santa Monica: Adizes Institute, 1977).

3   Ichak Adizes, *How to Solve the Mismanagement Crisis.*

4   Per Stewart Resnick, Chairman and President of The Franklin Mint. See quotation on back cover of this book.

5   Tom Monaghan with Robert Anderson, *Pizza Tiger* (New York: Random House, 1986).

6   Ichak Adizes, *Corporate Lifecycles.*

7   Jacques Ellul, *The Technological Society* (New York: Knopf, 1964).

8   Ichak Adizes and H.R. Haldeman, "Why Gorbachev Might Fail," working paper, Santa Monica: Adizes Institute, 1988.

9   H. Storm, *Seven Arrows* (New York: Harper & Row, 1972).

10 Ray Benson, *Relaxation Response* (New York: William Morrow, 1975).

11 Rabbi Harold S. Kushner, *When Bad Things Happen to Good People* (New York: Schocken Books, 1981).

Selected Previous Works by the Author
(available from the Adizes Institute)

Books

Corporate Lifecycles: How And Why Corporations Grow And Die And What To Do About It. Englewood Cliffs, NJ: Prentice Hall, 1988. Translated into five languages.

How To Solve The Mismanagement Crisis. Dow Jones/Irwin, 1979; reprinted by the Adizes Institute, 1980. Translated into thirteen languages.

With Elizabeth Mann–Borgese, *Self Management: New Dimensions To Democracy.* Santa Barbara, CA: ABC/CLIO and The Center For The Study Of Democratic Institutions, 1975; reprinted by the Adizes Institute, 1976.

Industrial Democracy: Yugoslav Style. New York, NY: Free Press, 1971; reprinted by the Adizes Institute, 1977. Translated into three languages.

Articles

With Paul Zukin, "A Management Approach To Health Planning In Developing Countries." *Health Care Management Review* 2 (Winter 1977): 19-37.

"Organizational Passages—Diagnosing And Treating LifeCycle Problems of Organizations." *Organizational Dynamics* (Summer 1979): 3-25.

"Mismanagement Styles." *California Management Review* 19 (Winter 1976): 5-20.

"The Cost Of Being An Artist: An Argument for the Public Support of the Arts." *California Management Review* 17 (Summer 1975): 80-84.

"Arts, Society And Administration: The Role And Training Of Arts Administrators." *Arts and Society* 10 (1974): 40-50.

"Boards Of Directors In The Performing Arts: A Managerial Analysis." *California Management Review* 15 (Winter, 1972): 109-117.

Working Papers

"The Common Principles Of Managing Oneself, A Family, A Corporation Or A Society" (1987).

With H. R. Haldeman, "Why Gorbachev Might Fail" (1988).

Yeheskel Hasenfeld, Ichak Adizes and Robert Chaffee: "Revitalizing Child Protective Services: An Organizational Change Strategy" (1988).

Audio and Video Programs by the Author

Audio Programs

- *Adizes Analysis of Management,* ManagersEdge Corp., Denver, CO (6 cassettes)

- *Adizes Analysis of Corporate Lifecycles,* ManagersEdge Corp., Denver, CO (6 cassettes)

- *Volume I, The Adizes Method: An Analysis of Management* (6 cassettes)

- *Volume II, The Adizes Method: An Analysis of Organizations* (6 cassettes)

- *Volume III, The Adizes Method: Team Building and Problem Solving* (5 cassettes)

Video Programs

- Program A: *Overview: The Adizes Process of Management* (3 tapes)
  "The Adizes Process of Management"
  "The Adizes Method: Questions and Answers #1"
  "The Adizes Method: Questions and Answers #2"

- Program B: *The Management Process* (4 tapes)
  #1. "The Roles of Management"
  #2. "Mismanagement Styles"
  #3. "Structural Causes of Deadwood"
  #4 "What is a Good Manager"

- Program C: *Organizational LifeCycles* (4 tapes)
  #5. "LifeCycles of Organizations: Growth Phases"
  #6. "LifeCycles of Organizations: Aging Phases"
  #7. "Analysis of LifeCycles"
  #8. "Treating the Growing and Aging Problems of Organizations"

- Program D: Decision Making and Implementation (2 tapes)
  #9. "CAPI: Predicting Managerial Effectiveness"
  #10. "Adizes Process of Decision Making"

All programs are available from the Adizes Institute and are published by the Adizes Institute, unless stated otherwise.

Other Works of Interest

The purpose of the following bibliography is to direct the interested reader to material by other authors that complements and supplements the contents of this book. I have not done a survey of the literature in this field. It was not one of the goals of this project. However, here are a few sources which I know are relevant.

- Abravavell, Elliot, M.D. *Body Type Program for Health, Fitness and Nutrition.* New York: Bantam Books, 1985.

- Alessandra, Anthony, and Wexler, Phillip S. *Non–Manipulative Selling.* San Diego: Courseware, 1979.

- Bell, Gerald *The Achievers.* Chapel Hill: Preston Hill, 1973.

- Bolton, Robert, and Bolton, Dorothy Grover *Social Style/Management Style— Developing Productive Work Relationships.* New York: American Management Association, 1984.

- Chopra, Deepak *Quantum Healing.* New York: Bantam Books, 1989.

- _____ *Creating Health.* Boston: Houghton Mifflin Co., 1987.

- _____ *Perfect Health.* New York: Harmony Books, 1990.

- Keegan, Warren J. *Judgement Choices And Decisions — Effective Management Through Self Knowledge.* New York: John Wiley & Sons, 1984.

- Keirsey, David and Bates, Marilyn *Please Understand Me: An Essay On Temperament Styles.* Del Mar: Prometheus Nemesis Books, 1978.

About the Adizes Institute

The Adizes Institute, established in 1975, is dedicated to researching, developing, applying and disseminating the Adizes methodology for mastering change: a holistic, systemic and participative methodology of mastering change with mutual trust and respect.

The Adizes School for Organizational Transformation, one of the branches of the Institute, trains, certifies, and licenses qualified Lecturers who are interested in teaching the Adizes theory, top executives who want to apply it in managing their own organizations, and leading consultants who want to transform organizational cultures to solve managerial problems.

Adizes Publications publishes books, manuals, audio and video tapes as well as a newsletter and working papers.

Adizes Associates, another branch of the Institute, is dedicated to the application of the Adizes methodology for mastering change. It provides consulting services worldwide.

For a list of publications, training programs, and consulting services, please write or call:

The Adizes Institute, Inc.
2001 Wilshire Boulevard
Santa Monica, CA 90403
Phone: (213) 453-5593
Fax: (213) 453-2866